The Missing Child in

Towards a Covenant Theory (

Family, Community, Welfare, and the Civic State

The Missing Child in Liberal Theory

Towards a Covenant Theory of
Family, Community, Welfare,
and the Civic State

John O'Neill

Published by the University of Toronto Press
in association with the Laidlaw Foundation

Toronto Buffalo London

© University of Toronto Press Incorporated 1994
Toronto Buffalo London
Printed in Canada

ISBN 0-8020-0627-2 (cloth)
ISBN 0-8020-7586-X (paper)

Printed on acid-free paper

Canadian Cataloguing in Publication Data

O'Neill, John, 1933–

The missing child in liberal theory

Includes bibliographical references and index.
ISBN 0-8020-0627-2 (bound). ISBN 0-8020-7586-X (pbk.)

1. Children – Government policy. 2. Children –
Government policy – Canada. 3. Child welfare.
4. Child welfare – Canada. 5. Family policy.
6. Family policy – Canada. I. Laidlaw Foundation.
II. Title.

HQ789.O54 1994   305.23   C94-931990-2

Contents

Foreword

In 1965 George Grant warned Canadians in *Lament for a Nation* that abandonment of tradition and common intent threatened the future of our nationhood. Canada could not persist if doctrines of autonomy, limited government, and submission to market forces were to prevail.

> No small country can depend for its existence on the loyalty of capitalists. International interests may require the sacrifice of the lesser loyalty of patriotism. Only in dominant nations is the loyalty of capitalists ensured. In such situations, their interests are tied to the strength and vigour of their empire. (69–70)

We are compelled to care about the well-being and prospects of other peoples' children as a condition of preserving our nationhood. If the value placed on national life recedes, displaced by an ethos of autonomy and dissociation, our relations with children and each other change profoundly. Children lose their collective status, and are no longer the ancestral and progenitorial bond of national continuity. Instead, they become private presences whose entry into the world is occasioned by the pursuit of private fulfilment. The child of choice becomes the responsibility of the adults who choose. The life quality and life chances for children increasingly reflect the arbitrary fortuities of family origins and biogenetic endowments.

With the decline of national concern for the well-being of children and youth, society is becoming a state arena for the protection and promotion of private interests. Other peoples' children now acquire the dissociated designations of 'resource' or 'risk.' As human resources, children are inducted and moulded into assets for productivity with the promise of private rewards for those who can provide the highest returns to employers in the global economy. Through risk assessment, clinicians promise early-warning systems to identify 'damaged' children of limited capital value, who are quickly inserted into the public economy of containment – treated, streamed, incarcerated, and eventually relegated to adult lives on the margins of domestic life. Youth of modest capabilities, earnest but not gifted, no longer find a middle world of basic comfort and security that accommodated the previous generation. Instead, as family providers, their prospects will depend upon contingent cycles of opportunity and vulnerability, periodically perched on the peripheries of the global economy or alternatively hovering above marginal subsistence.

It is nearly thirty years later, and George Grant's forebodings have become manifest in the political, intellectual, and fiscal depletion of the Canadian nation. Public confidence in the credibility of political authority has been denigrated through persistent portrayals of governments as corrupt, bloated, and inept. Advocates of popular sovereignty on both the left and the right, having discredited public institutions as bureaucratic and élite, insist on the higher legitimacy of raw sentiments crafted through polling and media coverage in defining the public good. The resistance of Canadians over the past two decades to paying the full cost of public programs has fuelled high interest charges on accumulated debts, and now paralyses the ability of governments in Canada to sustain current commitments and to act on emerging social requirements.

Nowhere is the incipient decline of Canadian nationhood more evident than in the neglect of the next generation. Canada has one of the highest rates of child poverty in the industrialized world, with nearly one in five children growing up under conditions of deprivation and exclusion. Young adults embarking on family formation and prospective parenthood face chronic levels of unemployment and underemployment, increasingly unable to establish basic foundations of economic sufficiency and security essential to sustain the commitments of family life. In the face of declining circumstances, we have been unable to mobilize national will to extend public support to families. To the contrary, billions of dollars have been removed from public contributions for the care of children since the late seventies, justified by the exigencies of fiscal debt and new doctrines of limited collective responsibility.

The industrialized countries of western Europe have also experienced stagnant economies and labour markets because of global restructuring. But they recognized the need to improve national supports to families with children. Family-allowance and child-benefit provisions have been increased to compensate for declining family wages. Child-support systems now recognize a collective responsibility to protect the living standards of children during periods of parental separation by means of public advances of private support payments. Child-care services have been expanded to stimulate the healthy development of young children and to support parental access to employment. European policies to support families recognize that collective contributions for the care of children are essential to national vitality.

The missing child in John O'Neill's essay reflects the loss of public will to sustain Canadian nationhood. Submission to market-generated values, perspectives, and imperatives has limited the scope of public options to care for children and sustain national continuity. O'Neill does not offer us a lament on the prospective disappearance of Canada. Instead, he issues a call to recast the ground of public discourse on the collective status of children and to recover Canadian traditions of common intent essential to sustain our nationhood into the next century.

O'Neill challenges contractarian precepts of the child, family, community, and the state as incompatible with an ethos of social care and continuity. A society that privatizes responsibility for the well-being of children treats families as social adversaries in competition for the polarized rewards of a market society. The state ceases to embody the principles of common intent, but is reduced to the role of mediator of private interests and intervenor to contain family risk and public instability. Police and prisons become the new imperatives of public spending, at the same time that fiscal virtue dictates that the provision of national staples such as schools, health care, and social insurances are pruned and privatized.

Liberal concepts of the individual as the primary unit of social experience place children in precarious states of vulnerability and risk in their daily lives. Families emerge as aggregates of autonomous individuals, whose stability and persistence are subject to the fulfilment of adult needs. Each participant, including the child, holds a growing portfolio of rights to be invoked during periods of distress or dissolution. Social and legal advocates can protect children from domestic abuse and violation, and can represent them at wardship and custody hearings. But they are powerless to assure the child of committed and caring family relations essential to healthy development. The world of individualized family life wedded to the contractarian ethos of market relations leads to a national life of minimalism, with reciprocity reduced to the calculus of advantage (utility) and the adjudication of claims (justice).

O'Neill proposes that we question prevailing assumptions of personhood. Children are born into the social membership of families and nations, whose traditions and commitments shape their life prospects. Children inherit the conditions of their sustenance and in turn are expected as adults to guard and enhance the bestowal of legacies to succeeding generations. These are not the market relations of trade and contract but the civic ties of transmission and covenant. O'Neill contends that deep layers of intergenerational responsibility and relation are at the foundation of nationhood, essential to the healthy development of children, and are recovered through an understanding of the civic commons.

O'Neill weaves the collective and personal dimensions of his civic perspective throughout the essay. The civic covenant is the affirmation and enactment over time of ties of mutual endowment and shared destiny animating all levels of social life. The covenantal child enters the world as the embodiment of legacy and continuity, in whose life resides the value of presence and passage. The covenant is rarely spoken, but is observed at milestone moments and affirmed through institutional and communal experiences and the daily enactment of family practices. Children in the civic commons grow up with assurances that other people care about their lives.

Families, communities, enterprises, and institutions are the embedded domains of the civic commons, the permeating social layers of the life world. Each domain makes a distinctive and essential contribution to national intent and vitality. In contrast to liberal views of pluralism, the domains are not autonomous sectors competing for advantage or national domination. The civic state is the stewardly presence in the commons affirming national values, sustaining public institutions, assuring the availability of basic staples, investing in economic capacity, and strengthening the generativity of each civic domain. The commons can accommodate diversity, including the presence of an active market sector, if there is a business class with loyalties to national vitality, committed and willing to contribute to civic life. Threatening to remove capital, export jobs, or leave the country if national policies do not submit to the advancement of business interests is incompatible with the ethos of the civic commons, and undermines the prospects for Canadian continuity.

O'Neill argues that the vital political question for Canada rests on whether we will recover the tradition of the commons, and survive, or fade as a nation and become a regional territory in the global market.

> What we must do in Canada is to understand that the liberal ideology has relocated itself in the global market and then we must reaffirm our own covenant ideology. We must refurnish the civic commons in our own response as a global people whose welfare is larger than its market assessment and whose accommodation of diversity among families, communities, religions, and schools is rooted in our historical and political will to survivance. In this covenant we are collected but not collectivized. The promise of Canada is personal not private; we answer it through one another because each of us has enjoyed the trust of every other and none is either above or beneath the civic condition we hold in common. (107)

This essay was commissioned by the Laidlaw Foundation of Toronto as a contribution to the work of its Children at Risk Programme. The Laidlaw Foundation has committed a significant portion of its resources over this decade to the development of new perspectives and strategies to advance the well-being of children in Canada, with a special concern for children growing up under conditions of economic deprivation, familial dislocation, and historical exclusion. As a result of research, consultations, and field projects of the program, the sources of risk to children have come to be understood as collective in origin, rooted in our inabilities to create national and local conditions conducive to the healthy development of children. It is not only the traditionally disadvantaged who are at risk, but growing numbers of the next generation who are vulnerable to lives of despair and diminished prospects.

The new conditions of risk flow from the loss of national commitments to children and family life, and the development of remedial rather than preventive approaches to care and support. The Laidlaw program has understood the need to examine the intellectual and cultural foundations governing our collective relations with children and our response to their circumstances. Dominant perspectives, sometimes designated as paradigms, shape commitments and strategies. As a result, conceptual elaboration has emerged as a vital dimension of Laidlaw work.

The program has adopted a life-chance perspective on child development to acquire a more comprehensive understanding of how forces and factors over time shape the well-being of children. This approach benefits from the findings of longitudinal studies that describe the ways in which converging clusters of environmental influence and personal capabilities determine how children proceed and progress through important periods of social change. Predictable transitions for children include the conditions of gestation and birth, the early years of active development, learning readiness to start school, the establishment of peer relations, movement through secondary education, and first experiences in the labour market. Less-predictable transitions can include family separation, the loss of parental employment, removal from the family of origin to surrogate care, an unexpected pregnancy, or conflict with the law.

Life assets are influences and capabilities that help children proceed proficiently through the expectations and experiences of transitions. Liabilities are forces and factors that hinder the process of transition and propel children into negative pathways of reduced life quality and diminished prospects. Life-chance perspectives focus on the public and private endowments of children and the social configurations of their assets and liabilities as they proceed through the developmental progressions of the life course.

John O'Neill's essay is the first in a series of Laidlaw publications to elaborate life-chance perspectives. He delineates the precarious prospects for children in a society of privatized endowments. A second essay in progress will define the co-requisites of life chances and examine civic approaches to the endowment of children. Monographs planned for the series include a review of the community-systems approach to social support for children and families, and a description of current work on social-indicator development.

MARVYN NOVICK*
13 June 1994

---

*Professor of Social Work, Ryerson Polytechnic University, and
Consultant, Laidlaw Foundation Children at Risk Programme

Acknowledgements

This study has benefited from close discussions with Marvyn Novick – with whom I have taken each step – and with Terry Sullivan, Robert Glossop, and my colleagues in the Children at Risk Programme of the Laidlaw Foundation. On their behalf I hope we have contributed to current policy debates something that will help us to confirm the assurances that every child asks of us not only in the International Year of the Family (1994) but every day.

The Missing Child in Liberal Theory

Towards a Covenant Theory of
Family, Community, Welfare, and the Civic State

ONE

A Duty-free Society?

It is time to reshape Canadian public discourse on the relation between the modern welfare state and the life chances of children born into families and communities at risk. The welfare state should not be sold off. Its covenant must be renewed if we mean to tackle the 'justice gap,' as it is now called in Britain (IPPR 1993). We must also resist the depletion and degradation of our civic institutions by any proposal to put a market price upon the staples of a good society. The current intensification of risks to families, children, and youth that derives from the globalization of market forces should not stampede us into stripping our civic institutions into lean and mean instruments of competition where self and community become ever-thinner concepts wasted by irresponsible greed and by privatization of the commons:

> What a community requires, as the word itself suggests, is a
> common culture, because, without it, it is not a community at
> all ... But a common culture cannot be created merely by
> desiring it. It rests upon economic foundations. It is incompat-
> ible with the existence of too violent a contrast between the
> economic standards and educational opportunities of different
> classes, for such a contrast has as its result, not a common
> culture, but servility or resentment, on the one hand, and

patronage or arrogance, on the other. It involves, in short, a large measure of economic equality – not necessarily, indeed, in respect of the pecuniary incomes of individuals, but of environment, of habits of life, of access to education and the means of civilization, of security and independence, and of the social consideration which equality in these matters usually carries with it. (Tawney 1931: 28–9).

It is time for Canadians to rethink the grounds of child, youth, and family security and to refurbish the institutions of civic sustainability that are richer than the forced choice of market or of welfare-state provision. The sustainability of civic institutions is enriched through an embodied tradition of obligations to one another that cannot be limited to contracts any more than it can be captured in the device of a safety net. Civic institutions are not created for any single purpose nor can they be exhausted in any single use. They do not belong to us except as an endowment that obligates us towards past and future generations, to whom we believe our present care of the civic commons to be owed. But the commons cannot be adequately funded where taxation is regarded as confiscation rather than embraced as the passage of obligation towards our civic others, whose lives are the absolute ground of our own and who thereby engage us in a covenant of life passage and tradition that far exceeds any calculus of return.

In the covenant view, families are not merely a by-product of individual lifestyles, because family life is the primary institution of infancy and childhood. Families make families. Families make communities. Communities make states. States should make sustainable communities and families that make and care for children and youth. Without such an overlapping framework of social provision, individual life chances are extremely limited even among those who believe that their wealth might buy off the inconveniences of an impoverished community. We are well aware that 'public familism' (Dizard and Gadlin 1992) now takes on two forms, one progressive but market-dependent, and the other regressive but equally market-dependent, inasmuch as many believe that families, schools, and universities are the proper source of successful recruits for the market. Whereas the progressivists invoke a 'thin' concept of state welfare, the regressivists invoke a 'thick' church-based supplement to family values. Whereas the progressivists regard contraception, abortion, sex education, and women's rights as essential elements in the contractarian reconstruction of the family, the regressivists are as opposed to these aims as they are to gay and lesbian rights, regarding them as equally anti-familist. In this regard, family values may be promoted by either side, while neither contemplates any civic investment that would sustain families in meeting social responsibilities that far exceed their individual capacity.

The lack of civic provision, of course, produces the very division between so-called good and bad families that is taken to justify the family-value controversy. It is essential not to constrain family history within any single period that might seem to offer us an ideal against which to measure contemporary failures. What we must ask ourselves is which families are most at risk in the market-place. We must ask which families are least able to indulge bourgeois ideologies of autonomy and dependence and most in need of the covenant provision we shall elaborate here in order to underwrite the social authority of families elsewhere than in the market. Above all, we must understand that families at risk are placed in danger by families of privilege who buy their labour cheaply and now threaten to buy their children.

In the new global economy, all nation-states are withdrawing the subsidies they once made to sustain family and civic institutions. Rather than accept this new conception of the 'leaner,' 'meaner' state as a model for the design of social agencies dictated by global capitalism, we must strenuously resist the notion that in ridding ourselves of the welfare state we would be freeing ourselves from an addiction to economic inefficiency and the destruction of family values. We should also reject any market device that recodes the income divide between families by drawing their children into a rainbow of complementary colours where class and racial differences appear to be erased. The concept of a covenant society must be understood independently of its economistic uses because we want to avoid speaking of 'deficits' where what is involved is injustice, exploitation, and the demoralization of sectors of the population who are in no way the 'material' or 'environment' of industrial activity except as their condition has fallen to inhuman levels. Unemployment, illness, racism, and exploitation are on a distinctively different level of conceptualization than global warming, ozone depletion, and deforestation. The 'greening' of the economy is a superficial response to sustainability, even at this level, since it is rarely incompatibile with profitability; for the same reason, 'green' represents a narrow band of nature's rainbow, once again compatible with the reduction of biodiversity in the interests of profitability.

The rhetoric of marketization, which many seek to introduce into public agencies, must not be allowed to veil the acceptance of scarcity and marginalization that now shapes our political problems. What Canada needs, against such trends, is an alternative vision of civic covenant and intergenerational justice as the proper legacy of families and of their children. Apart from such a covenant, the current language of social rights is likely to overburden state donations without due recognition of communitarian duties, or else to be drawn into marketized substitutions for social services delivered at the cost of large sectors of exclusion (Sullivan 1992; Trakman 1991). We must reaffirm the fundamentally historical and embodied ground of civic reciprocity that is beyond contract and sentiment, that recognizes no exclusion practices, and that is not bound by the moral vision of a single generation. We therefore reject the acceptance of an underclass in the current practices of the therapeutic agencies of public and private care. The practice of reciprocity in a modern society requires that we simultaneously refurbish the civic covenant and strengthen those agencies of a renewed welfare state that will link sustainable communities, families, children, and youth in ways that will reduce the risks of inequality of income, health, and education to which market society remains wedded.

In proposing a covenant concept of 'sustainable society' we want to bring the latter idea under the canopy of civic provision to remove it from its purely economizing and ecologizing constraints set out in the Club of Rome Report (Meadows 1972). Civic sustainability is broader than the fiscal and ecological practices of sustainable development. Ecologism is largely driven by contingent market forces. It involves one-way talk on behalf of mute environments that quickly reduces the complexity of civic responsibility from moral accountability to market accountability, which is then invoked as the real basis for political accountability. This conceptual slide moves us ever further from recovering the original civic covenant that is both embodied and embedded in everyday life. The responsibility of civic institutions for their troubles cannot be dictated by the global forces that now threaten to disengage themselves from any form of civic covenant. Thus, we do not understand civic sustainability to mean our ability to withstand the effects of the duty-free vagrancy of global corporations without the help of a positive concept of government.

We already know that the 'free trade' pacts of global capitalism demand that nation-states increasingly strip their civic institutions in order to compete with countries where the absence of welfare institutions offers a more 'hospitable' environment to civic-free global corporations. It is indeed a short-sighted innovation that asks us to strip our political history:

The arguments for a minimal state have never recommended themselves to any significant portion of mankind. Indeed, what

> is most common in the history of popular struggles is the
> demand not for deliverance but for performance: that the state
> actually serve the purposes it claims to serve, and that it do so
> for all its members. The political community grows by invasion
> as previously excluded groups, one after another – plebians,
> slaves, women, minorities of all sorts – demand their share of
> security and welfare. (Walzer 1983: 74)

Canada's political identity lies in its collective will to tolerate
higher marginal tax rates as the price for sustaining the civic
commons that has offered Canadians a more even playing field
than the market allows and that globalism will surely plough
under (Wolfe 1989; O'Connor 1989). The Canadian commons
derives from a concept of positive government that we must
save from the anti-governance of the market and its mythol-
ogies of voluntarism and communitarianism flourishing without the state (Putnam 1993). In this regard, too, we shall have
to be careful that we do not erode the civic commons through
rights-based claims of interest and minority groups that celebrate the voice of oppression/empowerment without regard
for the spread of opposition to government activity. To save
Canada's positive governance and its welfare covenant, we
shall always need a higher marginal rate of taxation for individuals and corporations than exists in the United States, with
due regard for the maintenance of the jobs and revenues from
which we draw the staples of citizenship. This is the fundamental policy principle that derives from the provision of
Canada's civic commons.

The state is not an alien force in our lives. Rather, the state
is merely our own will to achieve together what we have no
chance of accomplishing on our own. The welfare state does
not exploit us as much as we are exploited at work; the welfare state does not injure us as much as we are injured at
work; the welfare state does not make us as ignorant as the
commercial media that sell us our daily misinformation. The

welfare state does not enforce racism, sexism, and ageism; nor does it pollute the oceans, or extinguish animal and plant species. States are often murderous and oppressive, to be sure. But without the welfare state and its laws we have no way of responding to the forces of injustice and insanity that weaken the sustainability of our civic institutions. In the face of the forces that encourage the dissolution of the state as anything but a weak trade barrier and a willing debtor to patch up the social costs of global capitalism, we call for a second-generation welfare state in Canada whose task must be to guarantee sustainable institutions under the canopy of a civic covenant.

The Civic Covenant must be implemented on two levels:

a. social policy
b. welfare-state policy

Child risk programs must be focused upon family risk, and thus we place family policy at the heart of a second-generation welfare state policy (Krüsselberg 1987). What this means is that we are calling for a shift from a first-generation concept of social policy as the treatment of poverty in the interest of preserving the political order in a dual society (Muszynski 1991). The reduction of poverty will remain a function of any social policy. But since social policy tends to reduce welfare-state policy to such vexed issues as Who is poor?, How poor are the poor?, and Why aren't the poor motivated to work?, we believe welfare-state policy must be clearly distinguished from such troubles. What must be kept in focus is the question of how we are to implement welfare-state policy in regard to how the family (household) economy can be sustained in order to respond to the larger transformations of labour in the national economy and its global context. Moreover, this change in welfare-policy perspective demands that we think of the family economy in terms of both a 'cross-class' and an 'intergenerational' perspective, which we will sketch later on.

What must be kept in mind is that in the new global economy the old order's class-immunity breaks down – for example, in urban decay and violence that cannot be avoided, where the suburbs are also markets for drugs, and where television continuously feeds off the two economies of misery. Similarly, we can no longer throw the members of a family to their single-generation fate, since the maintenance of a family economy increasingly involves the interdependence of its pre-working, working – and out-of-work – as well as its post-working members. Of course, class, race, and gender variables complicate the family economy's life prospects. In drawing attention to the notion of the intergenerational economy, we are outlining an emerging political reality. Rather than invoke any normative family mode, we are placing emphasis upon the prospects for social well-being and social justice that would derive from a renewed family-economy approach to welfare-state policy. This is because the complexity of modern political economy places it so far beyond individual capacity and vision that only in the framework of a renewed welfare-state policy can 'human capital' be afforded its proper due vis-à-vis the global dominion of non-human capital. The global market trades off civic capital while increasingly adopting towards it what we have called a 'duty-free' policy. Civic-free global corporations, and not only governments, are to blame for the fiscal crisis that now threatens to erode any concept of the welfare state at the very moment when globalism forces us to renew our vision of welfare policy.

Market-driven society continuously violates its social contract with an underclass whose everyday life-world is ravaged, yet does not lead to any move by the poor to alter political apathy. Under these circumstances, the political self is 'thin' and dependent upon weak institutions that fail to refurbish the civic practices that would foster political solidarity. The result is a parasitical symbiosis between élite contentment and underclass dependency that is further undermined by the erosion of the welfare state, which is regarded as an act of public theft from the market-place on behalf of the ghetto of idleness, crime, and disease. While these arrangements are strange enough from the standpoint of the citizen-subject in a covenant society, they are even more alien to the children and youth who are hopelessly subject to such a contract. In reality, children and youth are absent from the social contract. Their life chances are pre-determined by the deadly odds in a society that renders health, education, and justice scarce commodities. As we shall see in the following chapter, it is only from the standpoint of the child that society appears to originate in a state of nature. But the child's aboriginal state is really a post-contractual effect of its parents' socio-economic circumstances and of their compounded effect upon the child's health and psychological ability.

A politics of civic presence (O'Neill 1985) must be recon-ceived as a repository of social and political obligation at every site where the family, children and youth, the sick and the aged, the unemployed, and the uneducated are engaged by the institutions of the market and the state. Without this insist-ence upon a politics of civic presence, grounded in our obliga-tion to solidarity, prior to any contractual consent and rights theory, we cannot hope to redeem the civic life-world merely through risk-management agencies. Without civic commitment, we cannot delimit the contingencies of the market-place that redefine otherwise inherent commitments as contracts and options, or as burdens or tax grabs imposed on a self-pos-sessed individual. Yet, curiously enough, it is the liberal insist-ence upon classlessness that in fact produces both the positive state it so abhors and the waves of populism it so fears. By contrast, because covenant theorists do not engage either the myth of classlessness or the myth of the withering away of the state, they are able to treat the recognition of differences as the basis for respect of persons in the conduct of the welfare-state covenant.

Covenant versus Market Concept of Institutions

Every day we experience shocks to our civic sensibility. In our view, these shocks are due to the *marketization of our social endowment*, of family life, of childhood, health, and knowledge, of security and employment. The raw side of the trend towards the marketization and defamilization of the social bond is what we see in street crime, drugs, school drop-outs, single-family poverty, homelessness, and unemployment, which we experience either directly or vicariously through media reportage whose power to observe is equalled only by its inability to explain. Indeed, the media coverage of the daily degradation of the life-world is itself an essential ingredient in the reduction of social concern to social anxiety that further undermines civility (O'Neill 1991). In these circumstances, social-policy thinkers have been forced to recognize that the current degradation of civic life requires us to recast political argument so as to modify liberal ideology with communitarian claims (Mulhall and Swift 1992). As a result, a liberal-communitarian consensus is being fashioned around the following propositions:

1 Communities shape individual decisions.
2 Communities provide goods that individuals could not provide for themselves.
3 Community institutions are better able than individuals to consider the historical long-run interests of individuals whose resources and foresight tend to be absorbed by immediate concerns.
4 Communities are more disposed to think in terms of ecological or contextual frameworks that capture the complexity of individual and social behaviour.
5 Communities (on many issues) are not less, and in fact are more, rational and compassionate than individuals.
6 Communities foster civility by weighing *both* moral com-

mitments and economic motives in the formulation of social policy.

From a Canadian perspective there is a noticeable lack of any positive concept of state agency in the liberal-communitarian platform, which remains decidedly 'American' in its commitment to mobilizing higher states of voluntarism in the market-place while hoping that despite its anti-statism it can produce a renaissance of civic virtue. Moreover, from a covenant standpoint, while it may be argued whether or not state agency weakens kin-community agency, it is evident that communitarian action without state involvement merely represents another version of voluntarism. In the end, liberal civility remains dependent upon a market agenda whose globalism is the mark of its virtually complete independence of state and community agendas.

In a recent communitarian debate concerned with the dilemmas of a 'duty-free' society – as we have put it – the spectre is raised that neo-liberalism may be in danger of exhausting its social capital (Putnam 1993), much as industrialization threatens to exhaust our natural environment. The concern is that the market imbalances rights and duties, aggravates private greed and public scarcity, and generates a fundamental confusion over what can be achieved on the level of self-interest and what is achievable through public association (Bellah et al. 1992). In short, the political contract that once underwrote market liberalism is virtually broken. Yet, into the very heart of this debate, Mary Ann Glendon introduces the claim that it is 'the family' that might be basic to the qualitative renewal of America's social capital:

One of the striking differences between the American Constitution and the constitutions of other modern democracies is that ours has no mention of the family ...

My language for Article I of a constitutional amendment on

family duty might be: 'The nation has a special responsibility for the protection and welfare of children and their families.' And Article II might read: 'The nurture and education of children are duties primarily incumbent on the parents.' (Marzorati et al. 1991: 47)

Glendon frames her two articles with a view to reversing the effects of family breakdown upon the social fabric of American society. She believes that these hortatory principles of law might have an educational effect upon market society. However, as Dan Kemmis points out in the discussion, any such hope of the law's effect is absolutely dependent upon the institution of intergenerationality:

> Any sense of duty ... has to draw upon the notion of connect-edness that is implicit in the idea of responsibility. When I was thinking about family and how we might impose a duty within a structure, I tried to imagine the family longitudinally - that is, between members of different generations. A duty to family or a duty to place must enjoin people to *remember* and to live in a way that deserves to be remembered and nurtures the practice of remembrance ... It is when we reaffirm that compact between ourselves and our progeny that duty is born. (ibid.: 54).

Nostalgia for past generations must, however, be given a positive civic state framework if the claims of intergenerationality are not to waste away in a noble but empty lament. Institutions, communities, and persons must be interpreted within a shaping environment of laws, governance, customs, rituals, rights, and responsibilities that, in the first place, constitute an *intergenerational covenant* enabling its contemporary usages, while secondarily imposing upon its legatories a *social debt* in regard of the reproduction and revision of the social legacy (Maciver 1920). This view is necessary in order to delimit our current possessive individualism (Macpherson 1962), as well as our current withdrawal from state governance, with a concept of *stewardship* exercised in regard of past and future generations and with renewed faith in everyone's ability to contribute towards the good society (see chapter 5).

Covenant versus Market Life Chances

It is time to expand the terms of the current liberal-communitarian debate and to argue for a shift from the *liberal contract paradigm*, with its minimalist assumptions regarding the noncontractual commitments of history, the state, community, and family, to a *covenant paradigm*, with maximum recognition of the social endowment that weaves individual, community, and state together in a shared civic culture whose reproduction is valued beyond the sub-utilities it generates in every other domain of life (*Social Well-Being* 1993). The contract paradigm originates in the fiction of a state of nature in which political actors are assumed to be already rational-utilitarians although disembodied, degendered, and unrestrained by family, as we shall show in our critique of Rawls in chapter 5. In the covenant paradigm, by contrast, we are born into a social commons whose usages can only be handed on but never owned or limited to anyone's grasp except as a violation of everyone's good. Properly speaking, this endowment cannot even be inherited, except as an obligation to serve it as stewards of this generation's indebtedness to past and future generations through whom social institutions derive their life, as we shall argue in chapter 3 (on family foundations).

The liberal-communitarian debate might also command our interest as part of the wider reformulation of a 'non-market theory of democracy' (Macpherson 1973). The latter involves an attempt to revise the assumption in liberal anthropology that individuals are exclusively utility-driven in favour of the broader assumption that individuals seek to develop essentially human talents in ways that are not inimical to each other's ability to do likewise. By the same token, this redefinition of individual and collective talents involves – in our terms – a shift from a contractarian to a covenant model of human agency, mediated by a positive concept of governance as the capacity not only to transform natural risks but also to transform civic relations. This shift would involve a greater recognition of our social indebtedness combined with social policies that will enhance everyone's life chances:

> If one wants to adopt a scheme of three layers, one can identify first of all *survival chances*: their elements are (at least) the obligations of the social contract and the welfare chances of a subsistence minimum. Survival chances offer elementary security. At the next stage, there are the *chances of a good life*, chances of prosperity or, with Smith, conveniency perhaps; they include religion and law as well as a considerable level of welfare and complex institutions. *Exceptional or privileged chances*, luxury chances perhaps entail on the other hand the highest level of options and ligatures attainable at a given time, those subtle linkages which the individual has creatively appropriated by understanding and activity, coupled with a barely restricted command over time and space. (Dahrendorf 1979: 77; my emphasis)

However, even Dahrendorf's anti-Darwinian formulation of life chances accepts that their fullest achievement lies either 'ahead' of or 'above' many people. Like many others, he is silent about children's life chances. By the same token, Dahrendorf builds into his implicit progressivism and estatism only a residual welfare factor to allay despair and discontent. What he does not say openly is that most people's life chances are governed by an *iron law of success/failure* which determines that most children will have to learn to endure the certainty of failure against the possibility that relatively fewer will succeed.

As we see it, market liberalism undermines the future of individual life chances because it also fails to foster the institutional chances of a good life. Indeed, it might be said that it is this inverted order of civic meaning and duty-free materialism (Wolfe 1989) that the liberal-communitarian debate struggles to revise. Yet, it is evident that where the civic staples of citizenship (health, education, and employment) are placed under the sign of scarcity, coded through the system of success and failure, then we seriously weaken the social covenant that underwrites all other contracts. Moreover, the harshness of these arrangements is aggravated by current corporate rhetoric that celebrates the 'greening' of natural risk while remaining indifferent to the proliferation and randomization of civic risks that plague the lives of families, schools, and cities whose resources are undermined and degraded by the 'civic-free' errancy of globalism.

However desperate civic life becomes for large sectors of liberal society, its political will to alter the suffering it spreads remains weak. Thus, Galbraith (1992) locates the liberal tolerance of public squalor in a dominant 'culture of contentment' simultaneously devoted to the privatization of wealth and a minimal welfare response to the underclass produced by its greedy arrangements. Galbraith's baptism of these conditions as a 'culture' exchanges irony for a flat insistence upon the division of liberal society into two worlds of naked wealth and bare poverty. Such irony, however, owes its effect to the remarkable political abstinence that is surely the return gift of the welfare poor (Pruger 1973). Despite the fact that in the United States the top 20 per cent of families enjoy 49.8 per cent of after-tax income, the empty-handed majority continue to dream the American dream any way they can. For, just as within the top income group a minority element of 1 per cent

FIGURE 1
Quintile distribution of income among families

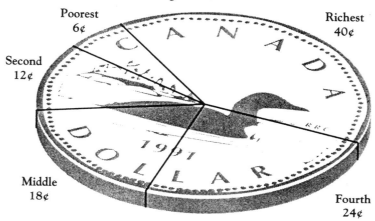

Poorest 6¢		Richest 40¢
Second 12¢		
Middle 18¢		Fourth 24¢

SOURCE: Statistics Canada, Income Distributions by Size in Canada, 1991

This Loonie shows the distribution of gross family income among equal 20% slices of the population (quintiles). The richest, or fifth, quintile contains the 20% of families with the highest incomes and the poorest, or first, quintile contains the 20% with the lowest incomes. Each of the five quintiles has an equal number of families in it.

In 1991, the richest quintile received 40 cents of every dollar of family income in the country, and the poorest quintile received 6 cents. In the past decade, the richest quintile has received an increasingly larger share of this dollar at the expense of middle and lower-income families. (Canadian Council on Social Development 1993a)

owns 12.8 per cent of national after-tax income, so at the bottom of the bottom 12.8 per cent of the population lives below the poverty line of $12,647 for a family of four (Galbraith 1992: 13–14). Similar arrangements prevail in Canada, as depicted in figure 1. To speak of these arrangements as a political culture is to adopt an exotic perspective upon the otherwise familiar effects of economic stratification in liberal society. It also requires a disregard of the civic risks that surround the ruling U.S. élite to call them a 'contented' majority (actually, they are a majority of the low-voting population), when what Galbraith means is that they are so shamelessly determined to preserve or extend their private privilege that they regard any taxation upon themselves as public theft. Here, in our view, is the hard rock of the 'duty-free society,' whose squalor and hazards are suffered by the poor, faced with the indifference of the wealthy who persist in disavowing any notion of social debt.

Covenant sociology rejects any sociology that hides the sub-contract of liberal democracy, namely, that no one shall totally reject the primary contract of competitiveness that produces a scarcity of success and an abundance of failure. Strictly speaking, the sub-contract of liberal democracy entails that *public issues be rendered private troubles* (Mills 1961; Merton 1963; O'Neill 1972), to be treated, for example, by privatized medical care and risk management that assume the incapacitation of a large sector of the populace. It is this version of the liberal social contract that we seek to reject in formulating the covenant paradigm of civic obligation as the ground of any adequate conceptualization of social care and its social-policy consequences in Canada.

In view of the current exhaustion of totalizing concepts of well-being and development, but faced with ever-expanding risks to which communities, families, children, and youth are exposed, Canadian social-policy research must reconceptualize the life chances and social pathways that enable/disable families, children, and youth in interaction with community and state institutions from which no one, however poor, should be excluded. Thus, it is necessary to examine how it is that 'the child' functions as a metaphor for our development, progress, and well-being, while simultaneously standing as a metaphor for the failure of society, for the inhumanity, poverty, and ignorance that stunts the lives of so many children (Hamburg 1992). Having in mind the institutional paradox figured in the child's innocence and suffering, in its promise and despair, we think it is necessary to link our conceptual approach to family, child, and youth *life chances* with a larger kin-community and welfare-state framework grounded in the notion of *social endowment*; that is, the reception, care, and handing-on of civic resources that facilitate early life chances in families and communities and strengthen their links to secondary institutions of school, work, and other social agencies.

The liberal consensus may be expressed in the following set of conflicting strategies that reproduce the marketization of family and child life chances in a dual economy of success-and-failure:

1 The marketization of the family
2 The femalization of child care
3 The therapeutic repair of family failure, disability, and de-moralization in place of an enabling social endowment that funds the civic debt which all citizens – without exclusion – hold in respect of one another:

Ad 1   It is essential to liberal ideology that the social world is atomic (Taylor 1979; Marquand 1988; O'Neill 1992) and that its individual members contract, copulate, and marry for reasons entirely of their own (Barber 1984). Families are regarded solely as private conveniences. To the extent that their members do well in the market-place, families can be expected to command the resources that enable them to carry out their 'natural' functions of reproduction and socialization as well as the promotion of their selfish interest in a certain level of public provision within their immediate community (see chapter 2).

Ad 2   The care of the young, sick, and elderly is largely women's work. Women are themselves both producers and consumers of such care. The ideological and economic degradation of gendered care (its femalization and privatization) deprives us of the recognition that the *moral economy of care* cannot be subordinated to the claims of justice in a developed civic community. Moreover, whatever factors contribute to de-skilling care by/and of women are absolutely detrimental to child care (see chapter 3).

Ad 3 While removing families from the public domain, the liberal enhancement of the economic resourcefulness of families demands that the families strive to meet market needs for healthy, educated, and employable citizens. In exchange for successfully honouring this implicit contract, market society permits the privatization of its rewards. Since the privatization of success results in the marginalization of failure, a professional therapeutic apparatus is obliged to contain the socio-psychological and potentially political consequences of the gap between the liberal ideology of success and its practice of failure.

What the liberal consensus obscures is that the market does not function to oppose 'opportunity' to 'risk' – as it might if its practices were indeed benevolent. What market liberalism sets at odds are *families of privilege* against *families of risk*. This dual economy of risk and privilege is privatized in liberal ideology to look as though it were a single economy populated by individuals who compete in a race whose rules fairly discriminate between winners and losers in such a way that no one is visibly a loser from the start. To sustain the illusion of equal starts, risk-management operations are introduced in order that infringements of the rules while the race is under way are 'corrected' to provide the effect of success according to natural ability (Goffman 1952). However, if we treat the track metaphor at all seriously, it is immediately obvious that most people at the track are gamblers but not winners. Yet it is no part of the pleasure of the sport to realize that the real winners are not those who enter but those who *own* the game:

In the Hobbesian race, many of the runners are running in
place, unable to break through the constraints of the larger
pattern. Nor can that pattern usefully be described as the product of their own valuations, a kind of social shorthand for the
recognition of individuals. There is indeed such a shorthand,
but it derives from the dominant ideology, itself a function of
office and power. (Walzer 1983: 256)

What is curious about the race image is even more strange
when it furnishes the organizing metaphor for the education of
our children and our own chances of health and employment
– of getting home safely. It then becomes clear that the liberal
race is not well suited to the human race since the market will
fail so many of us. Nevertheless, much of current talk about
global competitiveness results in the intensification of competition among the world's children in and out of school, in fac-
tories, in bondage, in armies, and in the sex trade (UNICEF
1990) – at the same time as large numbers of youth and older
workers are excluded from any participation in the economy.

Civic Sustainability versus Global Risk

It is essential to liberal metaphysics to believe that one person's determinism is another person's freedom. The forces that
remove one person's job elsewhere allegedly open up a job for
someone else. In the next round, the same forces will open up
opportunities for the first-round losers provided they relocate
and retrain to fit the new slots in the division of labour. Over
time, the market should so finely tune each person's function
that there is a perfect match between work demanded and
work supplied. In reality, market forces create far greater
dislocations in industries, occupations, families, and communities (Polyani 1944). Industries and towns die; individuals are
left permanently unemployed and families sink into poverty.
What was once a local effect produced within advanced indus-

trialized countries – and softened by comparison with their impoverished colonies – is now a global force impinging upon all national economies. Globalization is driven by corporations that consider themselves 'free' to exploit the most profitable combinations of high-tech investment and 'cheap' labour offered by countries that do not burden mobile corporations with the rates of taxation that underwrite the civic institutions of a sustainable society. But the nomadic corporation places national and regional governments in double fiscal jeopardy, since they are obliged to bear the costs of the social disloca-tion involved in globalization without adequate local compen-sation. Worse still, what the global élite refuses to pay in national taxation, it can buy at a profit by underwriting nation-al deficits. Here we have a powerful combination of forces that aggravate both intragenerational and intergenerational inequity and injustice.

How is it possible, then, that a world designed to give us our freedom and equality results in such great loss of freedom and such deep inequality? How is it possible that many nations, many communities and their families, and very many young people now fear the future that is currently in store for them? In effect, we are asking ourselves whether complex industrial societies can sustain a civic identity, marked by a concern for others and for the sustainability of the vast cultural and civic legacy we have received from our ancestors.

What is currently happening to recontextualize the question of collective reasonableness and civic justice is that the condi-tions of wealth production, consumption, and redistribution are now subordinated to a new model of risk production (Beck 1992) as the dominant mode of wealth creation, whatever the costs to the sustainability of civic and personal identities. At first sight, such a notion flies in the face of the technological certainty that underwrites modern assurance. Surely, our indus-trial civilization has removed us from those natural risks to life and limb that characterize pre-industrial societies, whose contemporary famines and diseases serve to remind us of miseries beyond which we have advanced. If there are dangers in modern living, they are, so to speak, existential risks that we freely entertain in the pursuit of autonomy. For the rest, we believe that modern technology has so reduced the probability of any risk in its usage that it would be irrational not to use airplanes, automobiles, medicine, and microwaves for fear that they would be harmful in our particular employment of them. Such a fear would encourage the return of magic. It would constitute an abandonment of our technological faith in the probable security it otherwise delivers us. Worse still, it would return us to poverty and the lash of every natural disaster.

What we have now to contemplate is an extraordinary shift in the ratio between wealth production and risk reduction. Whereas historically we have produced wealth with the result that life has generally become more comfortable, longer, and more healthy – even when dangerous occupations are taken into account – *we are now faced with the emergence of an economy whose production of risk is endemic to its production of wealth.* Before looking into the details of this structural shift in modern political economy, we must underline that it involves a simultaneous shift in the welfare models of advanced industrial societies (Korpi 1983). We may express this shift in the following diagram, which also expresses the overlay of the two economies of wealth and civic risk as they in turn bear upon any ethical concept of welfare as well as our own proposal for the renewal of sustainable civility:

1 *Wealth production under national capitalism*
  Natural risk reduction + Social-welfare repairs
2 *Risk production under global capitalism*
  Increased civic risk + Reduced social-welfare repairs
3 *Civic sustainability*
  Social-welfare endowments and reduced civic risks

It might be said that early-modern industrial society had to learn to repair the natural risks incurred by its technological apparatus as well as devise welfare schemes to reduce the civic risks endemic to its class/property apparatus. However, while we are still concerned to tinker with the industrial and social risks engendered by a wealth-driven political economy, we now have to learn how to repair the huge risks to sustainable civic institutions that are incurred by wealth production in the global economy. But this means we must extend – rather than reduce – the welfare state to include the reduction of ill-health generated not only by the self-contaminating products and hazards of global industrialism but also by its dereliction of civic responsibility:

> For what we do when we declare this or that good to be a *needed good* is to block or constrain its free exchange. We also block any other distributive procedure that doesn't attend to need – popular election, meritocratic competition, personal or familial preference, and so on. But the market is ... the chief rival of the sphere of security and welfare; and it is most importantly the market that is pre-empted by the welfare state. Needed goods cannot be left to the whim, or distributed in the interest, of some powerful group of owners or practioners. (Walzer 1983: 89)

We are now forced to reconsider the principles of social welfare not only in terms of the redistribution of wealth but also in terms of the redistribution of risks that affect the sustainability of civic institutions. This, then, is the broader framework of any adequate concept of risk in respect of the world's children and their families. It is possible that this global framework of risk may induce a certain solidarity between adults, children, and youth. Whereas in class terms *some* are never afflicted by the risks of poverty, *no one* escapes the afflictions of globalized risks to our air, water, food chain, forests, and heavens. Having said this, we have still to rework our cognitive and moral maps to rethink civic sustainability rather than continue to rely upon scarcity-thinking to ration out the unequal risks of the emerging global economy of industrialized hazards. In this process we are obliged to *globalize our moral maps* since it is increasingly impossible to set up national and class walls to protect privileged moral environments. It necessarily follows that the moral environment of children can no longer be isolated. We can no longer imagine childhood as a pre-political or pre-economic realm safe from the hazards of the adult world without indulging a fantasy of child-immunity that is constantly violated through the intrusions of generation, class, race, and nation. Nor can we reasonably treat the middle levels of privilege in industrial societies as the normative environment for every other underprivileged group either within industrial democracies or outside of them.

We must rethink the concept of sustainability because the new industrial globalism is its own environment for the production of major hazards to its own civic sustainability. The self-infliction of global risk is the defining feature of the new world industrial order. Of course, a society that produces its own risks will produce its own *ideologies of natural risk* as a positive enterprise inclusive of its own risk-reduction and risk-redistributive discourses. These ideologies of natural risk are designed to socialize (but not to civilize) catastrophes such as earthquakes, famines, oil spills, and refugee movements. The naturalization of risk increases our ignorance of global risk-production. Against this, we must understand that

1 the reduction of natural risk is produced in accordance with existing class and race differentials;
2 civic risks are increasingly produced hazards that also intensify class and race differentials;

3 risk-management techniques treat violations of civic trust as natural necessities; and
4 the corporate globalization of risk as natural necessity reduces the citizen to passive adaptation in the face of natural necessity.

The combined effects of these discursive strategies is to control the redefinition of industrial (ir)responsibility in the risk society without courting any major political limitation upon the very corporate agents that continuously undermine the sustainability of civic institutions.

Social policy will flounder unless its producers know what it is they want (Maxwell 1993). Without an adequate concept of sustainable institutions to guide policy practitioners, we are obliged to treat whatever they do as what we want. The disappointment that ensues from the lack of any fit between social vision and social practice is, of course, easily reduced by the hardened practitioner's commitment to realism, if not boredom. Under these circumstances, political realism hardly amounts to more than a willingness to compromise with the trade-offs that result in the institutional degradation that surrounds us.

We currently lack any grand idea of civic sustainability. We do so, however, not from sharing the failure of nerve that now rules in the minoritarianism of the arts and social sciences that has captured legal and academic institutions and rattled the media. We lack a grand concept of sustainable society because we are unwilling to recognize the unity of the civic-free global forces that throw up the world's refugees and migrants and unmoor the world's cultures and cities wherever globalism reaches. Instead, we set ourselves the task of living without identities, without families, and without governments in order to accommodate a globalism that has in fact done more than its postmodern celebrants to oblige us to rethink how we can underwrite the sustainability of our civic institutions.

Canada's Civic Covenant

In Canada our traditions of social care, global economic cycles, and right- and left-wing politics, on both federal and provincial levels, constitute an ever-changing context of definition and redefinition in our concepts of rights and responsibilities, state welfare, endowment, stewardship, and community (Cragg 1986; Banting 1987). Whatever circumstances inspire rethinking the Canadian concept of social welfare, it must be taken as axiomatic that our deliberations are not rendered more 'rational' by being placed under the sign of 'scarcity' (Dryzek and Goodin 1986) any more than they are better pursued through the litigation of rights that derive from anti-governance. In the first place, our economic institutions are themselves dependent upon other social and political-legal institutions to make operative their own scarcity rules. And, second, economic rationality, so far from being the source of other rational conduct, is itself hugely subsidized by the reasonable, moral, and just institutions that provide the civic framework of any political economy. Third, no advanced industrial economy entirely disavows its production of social inequality and the consequent necessity to make state provision, on the one hand, for vulnerable groups (children, youth, elders, the unemployed, the sick, the handicapped) and, on the other hand, to ensure certain basic 'civic staples' – health, education, employment, law and order.

In Canada we are inclined to include in our concept of political economy a concern for the distribution of income, not only between capital and labour but also between age, gender and regional groups (Osberg 1990). We are therefore concerned to promote anti-discrimination legislation to reduce inequities on the level of individual income while also promoting social policies that reduce inequity between social classes, families, and regions of Canada. It is, however, essential to avoid a negative-liberties concept of our recent Charter of Rights:

Charter liberalism unduly circumscribes social practice. In particular, it imposes the personality of the abstract right-holder upon groups – upon Catholics and Protestants, rich and poor, men and women alike. In protecting the rights of the self-directed individual who holds herself out against a single foe, the state, *Charter* interpreters bypass the identity crisis of groups within the Canadian polity. They concentrate upon conflicts between individuals and government. They pass over social issues that transcend both. (Trakman 1991: 1)

We propose to capture what we think is the national consensus at both the federal and provincial levels of government in Canada in our own concept of civic covenant (see chapter 6). Although we insist that the Canadian civic covenant is not a scarcity-driven concept, we do not ignore the central fact of structural unemployment and the increasing immiseration of the working poor reported in *Perspective 2000* (Canadian Council on Social Development 1988). It is also quite evident from the *Countdown 93: Campaign 2000 Child Poverty Indicator Report* (Canadian Council on Social Development 1993b) that a diminished future awaits our children and youth unless we rethink our concept of the welfare state. For it must not be assumed that the civic-free global economy will in any way alter the pattern of inequality within and between industries – in fact, it is already clear that it aggravates the social division between the rich and the poor, as well as between the young and the old. The danger of any fragmentary political response to globalism is that we shall allow ourselves to be consumed with equity issues litigated between the sexes, generations, and races at the expense of the larger question of reworking the foundations of a sustainable society in the very context of greedy globalism and two North American free-trade pacts.

Here one thing should be certain. Canadians very well understand that there is a definite relation between social health and economic vitality, as is evident from the recent report of the National Forum on Family Security (Keating and Mustard 1993). Indeed, they do so better than many of our politicians whose position on this issue causes such frustration in the electorate. This is not only because all Canadians seek access to good medical practice, but also because they understand that they cannot be healthy in a society that is ravaged by unemployment, crime, and prejudice (Hertzman 1990). It is this larger concept of the civic covenant and its welfare-state apparatus that we will elaborate – keeping in mind our mandate to focus upon how children and the youth of today and tomorrow are doubly jeopardized by the failure of their elders to bequeath them an adequate social legacy in the form of a sustainable society whose institutions may civilize their hopes, removing them from the pact of servility and arrogance by dedicating them to mutual service and community.

In a *covenant democracy* we would favour the common legacy of an enabling social endowment for the development of individual differences whose relative worth is expressed in a market that we recognize must itself be subject to socio-legal constraints upon its tendency to over- or under-value individuals but, even more so, to put at risk the necessary 'commons' presupposed in all civic activity. Canada's commitment to the funding of the institutional commons and the social endowment through which we underwrite every citizen's life chances must not be placed under 'the sign of scarcity' defined solely by the market. Rather, our civic institutions must be regarded as an inalienable source of stewardship and care embraced between generations in which no one is too poor to contribute something of themselves and to others. In short, a democratic society must now think of its citizens in terms of a set of sustaining civic institutions that

1 operate as an enabling *social endowment* upon which individuals may build in accordance with their particular developed abilities and future life chances;

2 uphold an ethical and political discourse upon citizens' rights and responsibilities that constitutes a *civic covenant* from which no one – and no underclass – is excluded;
3 underwrite the *life chances* of all families, children, and youth in respect of their physical and emotional well-being, taking into account a variety of parental settings; and
4 counter the possibility that the present generation is renouncing its *social debt towards future generations* in favour of market and privatized models of care and disability.

Recently, the broad assumption of a civic covenant that we have just sketched has been put in question with regard to whether it is better furnished by the state in a substantive mode or as a formal framework with market provision (Taylor-Gooby 1991). Thus, the state is rejected as an outdated, patriarchal, if not blind, bureaucratic institution whose provision of goods and services produces dependency and amoralism in an underclass that weakens democracy and civil society. By contrast, it is argued that the reduction of state-administered social welfare to a formal framework of rights would revivify market, family, and community institutions as providers of social care consonant with a consumer-sovereignty model of citizenship.

We must reject this crude alternative. In Canada we have enjoyed many of the basic staples of a good society through state provision, for which we should gladly tax ourselves. We are quite aware that there exist complex arguments around the concept of welfare citizenship (Heclo 1986; Turner 1986; Roche 1992) that should be analysed for their relevance to Canada's history and current rethinking of its notions of citizen rights and responsibilities, personal autonomy, social needs, and of market, voluntary, and community delivery systems of care (Valpy 1993). Particular attention must be given to the articulation of the fundamental assumptions underlying the Canadian covenant so that they are not too easily set aside in favour of the alleged realities of the global economy that are invoked to whittle down state provision of welfare goods and services (Hunsley 1992). Attention must also be given to the unintended consequences of 'welfarism' to the extent that it undermines the social cohesion and moral chances of social groups it was hoped would be fostered by our programs of social welfare (Drover and Kerans 1993). However, these arguments must not be pursued apart from consideration of the fundamental structural shift in employment sectors of the economy that produces the de-skilling, 'femalization,' and 'childing' of the labour force, accompanied by the 'femalization' and 'childing' of single-parent-family poverty (McDaniel 1993). These phenomena require innovative state-welfare responses (including accountability) rather than acceptance of the end of welfare, which would surely increase social misery:

> The significant feature in the history of the social services is not the magnitude of the redistribution of wealth effected by them. It is the magnitude of the results which even a slender and reluctant redistribution has been sufficient to produce. Inequalities of health, of educational opportunity remain appalling. But it is not a small thing that certain diseases should have been virtually wiped out ... that some measure of educational provision, cramped and meagre though it is, should be made for all children ... and that the tragedies of sickness, of age and unemployment should have been somewhat mitigated. Compared with what might be accomplished, these achievements appear trivial. Compared with the actual conditions of a generation ago, they represent the first harvest of a policy, tardily adopted and persistently sabotaged, which, if resolutely pursued, can make the essentials of civilization a common possession (Tawney 1931: 145).

In speaking of the basic staples of the civic covenant, then,

we have in mind a number of citizen supports whose unconditional presence is enjoyed not only as a matter of entitlement
but also with positive state obligation to sustain them on
behalf of future generations. Canadians do not regard such
staples as health, justice, security, education, and employment
as market prizes to be enjoyed despite their unavailability to
large numbers of their fellow citizens. Nor should the provision of these civic staples be deeply stratified like any other
commodity in the market-place: the health, education, and
security of each Canadian is the health, education, and security
of all Canadians. For we think it is entirely false to the history
of state welfare to say that the state cannot provide good
libraries, good schools, good cities, good health, and good
insurance. To deny that the welfare state has enabled the lives
of millions of young people and elders without producing
dependency and disability among them is to deny much of the
goodness of the good society as we have known it in the
twentieth century.

TWO

Children in the State of Nature:
The Missing Link in Liberal Theory

We have reviewed the prospect of a 'duty-free' society in order to show that it involves a number of self-contradictions, even though in many ways it captures the essence of market liberalism and its surrender to civic-free globalism.

It is essential to liberal contract theory that individuals not be handicapped by the past-and-future effects of their disadvantage and vulnerability in the market-place. Liberal theory also minimizes the role of the state upon which liberal society nevertheless relies to contain its civic discontent and to provide a measure of peace and order. Despite the fact that the state is heavily involved in police and welfare activities to patch up the endemic troubles that derive from intra- and intergenerational poverty, unemployment, illness, crime, and urban decay, political liberals nevertheless regard the payment of those taxes necessary to preserve a minimum of civil security as a further threat to property and privilege. Indeed, rather than address the structural failures of liberal society, its libertarian ideologists prefer citizens to run the social and psychic risks of trying to live with the dysfunctions of the market society by treating the incidence of crime, disease, and failure reported in the media as random events. This is an essential device in the moralization of the differential costs and rewards of wealth and poverty. The preservation of the ideology of random crime results in huge enforcement costs to police and imprisons hundreds of thousands who offend the order between rich and poor. At the same time, the state's failures provide a justification for the very notion of a 'duty free' society that is the source of these troubles, inasmuch as individuals imagine they can 'buy out' from the dangers of the city, from poor schools and housing – but especially from medical neglect and exposure to the various illnesses that ravage large sectors of the population. To the extent that privileged sectors of market society conceive of contracting out from the provision of civic staples by the purchase of marketized services, the forces abound that weaken governments, communities, and families, that put at high risk children and single mothers, that aggravate racism, sexism, and ageism.

We must counteract the unethical notion of a duty-free society with a forcible restatement of the claims upon us of reciprocity and covenant care as the vital springs of a sustainable society. In this chapter, these issues are approached from the standpoint of how we are responsible for extraordinary high-risk concepts of childhood, as well as of family and community impoverishment, whose cumulative effects upon disadvantaged children and youth must constitute an unavoidable social-policy focus in any attempt to rethink a sustainable society with a strong second-generation concept of the welfare state. Therefore, we want to draw attention to the paradox of 'the missing child' in liberal social theory. The point of this device is to make it clear that, in the covenant perspective, the subject of politics is only properly conceived when the political subject is recognized as an embodied, gendered family-subject whose reciprocal regard for other citizens is constitutive of one's moral worth and civic agency. Thus, we must treat the child as a political subject. We do so not from a child-rights standpoint, but because the commitment of the children of our own generation, as well as of future generations, to a class contract that is so inimical to their well-being invalidates the moral grounds of market society.

The liberal contract is a contract to pit children against one another so that their hunger, their ignorance, their abuse, and the hopelessness of their lives is either to be regarded as their own bad luck or as the ordinary outcome of their parents' failures. The sight of such children – to whom our schools will also turn a blind eye wherever the competitive curriculum is enforced – represents the greatest violation of the covenant body shared by us and our children. Such a curriculum also violates our schools as civic institutions whose collective gift to our children stands, in the first place, to offer them the civic assurance that they have not left home only to get lost on the way to the market-place for which the grade school is merely a service station. By the same token, violence *in* our schools must be regarded as a civic violation *of* our schools. On the covenant view, the child's civic life is already guaranteed in our schools, parks, libraries, streets, and municipalities, which sustain the growth of the child into civic citizenship. But all of this cannot hinge upon the thin devices of IQ and grades. It turns upon the milieux of civility and security that are the daily provisions of a civic society through its schools, libraries, theatres, parks, and playgrounds.

The more disadvantaged, de-skilled, and diseased the parents to whom a child is born, and the less stable their family, community, and state environment, the greater are the risks imposed upon children and youth. The core of child risk, then, is to be found in the vastly unequal family environments into which children are born. Poverty strikes at the bio-psychic chances of a child as well as its socio-economic life-chances. Poverty may indeed produce 'poor children' as well as children who are poor (Hertzman 1990). Such is the intergenerational risk whose injustice we believe can only be reduced and removed by a covenant of care between families, communities, and welfare-state agencies. Here Canada has much to do as

FIGURE 2
Infant mortality rates in poor and rich neighbourhoods, 1971 and 1986

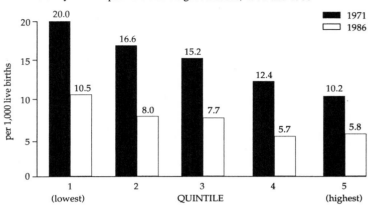

SOURCE: Wilkins et al., Statistics Canada, *Health Reports*, Vol. 1, no. 2, 1989

may be seen from figure 2, which shows that, while we have reduced overall infant mortality between 1971 and 1986, nevertheless infants in low-income neighbourhoods are twice as likely to die in their first year of life – not to mention their shorter life span and initial disadvantages of premature birth and low birth weight, which limit later development.

A civic society is marked by its horror of the missing child just as it is shamed by the homeless and the refugee. No one can be excluded from civil society unless its covenant of care has been degraded along with the other inconveniences of incivility. Imagine what is conveyed to a child through the adult focus of liberal anthropology. It would have to believe that its elders have never been born, had never lived as children, and would not age or die. The child's own condition would be a mystery to it, since it is obliged nevertheless to interpret the world with its body, to wonder whether it will be fed and loved, whether it will be protected or exposed to harm, whether it will thrive or be sickly. At the same time, the child would learn that infants are aborted, starved, drugged, battered, abused, and murdered. It would know that children are crippled, enslaved, sold into prostitution, and enlisted in armies (Ressler 1993). Yet the child's hopes for improvement in its own condition would depend upon an adult conception of social and political life in which the principal actors are disembodied, defamilized, and degendered individuals without any regard for intergenerational justice (Elshtain 1990a).

The child has no 'theoretical home' in liberal political anthropology (Etzioni 1988: 157). How, then, can we bring the child into our founding concepts of social and political theory rather than continue to assume that the child's place is provided for in liberal social theory? It is evident that liberal theorists are incapable of extracting civic institutions from a pre-social state of nature once their base assumptions are exposed:

1 The liberal contract is ahistorical and is unreal in its assumptions about community and individual behaviour.
2 Liberal anthropology assumes that its individual agents are disembodied, degendered, and defamilied.
3 As a consequence of (2), the constitutive character of the political subject of contract theory is empty, and as such provides no grounds for political choice.
4 Furthermore, the liberal-contractarian distinction between private and public life empties both domains, since the private domain is inhabited by disembodied entities (2 and 3 above) that can make no claims upon the political domain.
5 In short, liberal anthropology is incapable of furnishing the ontological grounds of social and political embodiment (O'Neill 1985).

Although liberal atomism appears to break the bonds of patriarchy, whether between man and god or between men and women (once in the same class as children and slaves), in fact the individual autonomy that Newton, Hobbes, and Descartes each sought to ground is as little suited to the grammar of knowledge as it is to the grammar of social life (O'Neill 1989). We cannot properly understand individual behaviour apart from the socio-structural background that it presumes for its own 'evidence' or 'normalcy.' By contrast, liberal atomism requires that individuals be considered absolutely independent of their institutional contexts so that each can freely move in an entirely homogenized space of equality. In short, the liberal political subject is constituted in total isolation, while liberal 'society' is correspondingly constituted through the total exchangeability of its atomic subjects. Paradoxically, the grammar of atomism is only complete in an homogenized or totalitarian state that merely renders explicit on the level of politics what is implicit on the level of market society. But this paradox can only be understood in an alternative language of covenant and social justice where self-interest is not the motor-force of social life.

The language of covenant and obligation offers an alternative account of the dedication of individual and collective life without the fictions of rationalized interests or of the contractually limited origins and ends of our institutional commitments. What is affirmed in the civic covenant is a historical legacy that is the organizing principle for the flourishing of differences that are sustained without being subject to the contingency of consent. We do not consent to Remembrance Day. Rather, people of every sort, of every age and place, wear the red poppy and are silent for a minute or two in recollection of an incalculable loss that is the inexhaustible gift from one generation to another. We do not consent to the founding principle that the family is not grounded in itself but is constituted through its relation to the continuance of every other family. Here the covenant principle of intergenerationality organizes all other family contracts without itself being subject to them, as we shall see in the next chapter. By the same token, the principle of intergenerationality allows us to see that, whatever the secular variants of family structure, the institution of the family cannot be subject solely to the will of a particular family that considers itself the convenience of its contracting parties. The contract family in effect condemns children to the fiction of a start to which they were never partner. Rather, as children, they are the very limit of the notion of marriage based upon sexual contract.

Liberal theorists experience great difficulty in accommodating the family and the child in their political discourse:

> For many reasons ... children have been the companions of women in the closet of political science. A few short years ago women began to set up such a clamour that a few were released ... Children remain, with few exceptions, both silent and invisible – relegated to a conceptual space (which is presumed to reflect social reality) that has been declared apolitical. *The political study of childhood remains in its infancy.* (Elshtain 1982: 289; my emphasis)

Contract theorists from Hobbes to Rawls have assumed that the child is entirely in the power of its male parent (Pateman 1988). This assumption is further aggravated by the exclusion of the female parent from the public domain. Contract theory – which Benjamin Barber (1984: 40) has described as 'zookeeping' – operates in the fraternal order where what males have to fear is one another. Here 'their' women and children are sources of either pride or shame, best experienced in domesticity, but to be excluded at all costs from the domain of politics:

> This is a strange world: it is one in which individuals are grown up before they have been born; in which boys are men before they have been children; in a world where neither mother, nor sister, nor wife exist. The question is less what Hobbes says about men and women, or what Rousseau sees the role of Sophie to be in Emile's education. The point is that in this

universe, the experience of the early modern female has no place. Women are simply what men are not. Women are not autonomous, independent, and aggressive but nurturant, not competitive but giving, not public but private. (Benhabib 1987: 162)

In fact, contract theorists espouse a virgin myth of the individual citizen as 'one' who exits from the state of nature into society through an act of will, contracting into a superordinate political authority. Thus, the political subject of liberal theory is disembodied, dispassionate, defamilied, and degendered as a precondition for exercising the political virtues of generalization and impartiality that would otherwise be contaminated by the particularities and affections of an embodied subject whose social bonds both delimit and enable political conduct:

All interests, values and conceptions of the good are open to the Rawlsian self, so long as they can be cast as the interests of a subject individuated in advance and given prior to its ends, so long, that is, as they describe the objects I seek rather than the subject I am ... It rules out the possibility of any attachment (or obsession) able to reach beyond our values and sentiments to engage our identity itself ... And it rules out the possibility that common purposes and ends could inspire more or less expansive self-understandings and so define a community in the constitutive sense, a community describing the subject and not just the objects of shared aspirations. (Sandel 1982: 61–2)

Without the very embodied subjects overlooked in liberal metaphysics, our ethical and political choices would be entirely without context or purpose, as we shall see in chapter 5 where we comment upon Rawls's concept of justice. By contrast, in a covenant theory of the state and community it is recognized that gender, age, infirmity, health, intelligence, and strength are the very elements of moral and political life, and require of us a judicious weighting of the moral contributions of both justice and care in dealing with one another. In the covenant view of things, gender and family may contribute to social policy, just as much as the views of the 'impartial' or 'bureaucratic' decision-maker. This is *not* because gender and family are finer, or more intuitive, but because they are civic in their nature, never having expressed a claim that was not relative to the claims of surrounding kin and community.

Yet the family covenant is not a tribal retreat into ethnicity or into religion. It is, rather, the uninhabitability of market society that reproduces the retreats of tribalism, of sects, and of those violent ghettos that so disturb the liberal conscience. But the same will be true wherever we fail to set forth a civic socialism to defend the everyday life-world, which will respond to abandonment either in retreatism or else by going underground to wait out the winter of its discontent, as has happened throughout history. The life-world has always offered our humanity such underground retreats from where, from time to time, there erupt great struggles against the pathologies of politics and the market.

The Game of Inequality

In covenant theory we cannot think of children without think- ing of families and communities. But in liberal contract theory we do not think of families because we think only in terms of disembodied individuals. This makes it even harder to think of children. It also makes it difficult to think of class, race, sex- ism, and ageism except as slight obstacles in the path of indi- viduals. Yet individuals are not really blind to the social insti- tutions that reproduce their differences in endowment and achievement. Rather, in liberal ideology individuals are led to think of their lives as entered in a race in which the finishing line is at the end of the run and the starting line as straight as possible. Market society is so enamoured of competition that its members believe that the odds are always in their own favour at the outset – or at least can be made to appear so with some slight handicapping of anyone else's outstanding advantages that threaten to make the outcome of the competition depressingly evident from the start. In such a society, schoolchildren are thought of as the happy entrants in its game of opportunity. Here, although each child is as lovely as another, each one may become more lovely, more healthy, more intelligent, more happy, more housed, more fed, and more amused, and each child *more* than another, however this may leave the other child so little of a childhood as to be virtually out of the game by which all their other games are measured. Nothing, then, is taken more seriously in liberal society than the child's initiation into educational rites that celebrate its happy acceptance of the equal playground upon which it will learn the game of inequality.

From the covenant perspective, it is children who are the ignored tokens in the move from the pre-social state of nature to the state of liberal society. Children are not individuals from the start. They have to be apprenticed in their families and schools to the rules of the game of competitive individualism. In liberal society, however, children are equal only to the extent that their families are sufficiently equal to apprentice them to a good enough start in the game of inequality (Jencks et al. 1972; Coleman et al. 1982). The evidence of this circumstance is all around us. Yet we still sentimentalize the horror of our practices of rendering our children poor, unhealthy, ignorant, and unloved. We imagine that such injustice can only be accounted for by the absence of an ideal start in life. But the truth is that we believe in an ideal start that would prepare children for their unequal results in a competition whose next rounds result in the *intergenerational inequality*, injustice, and ignorance that sets the floor of market society – if not a trap-door through which so many children fall into oblivion.

Just as we like to imagine equality as the initial state of children, so we like to think of freedom as the state of children and youth before they assume the burden of institutions in later life. But since in liberal society formal freedom of opportunity is more valued than equality of chances, children are doubly subject to the lack of freedom and equality that marks their family position. While we cannot totally ignore the larger forces that determine class and status (Dahrendorf 1959), here we are concerned only with the relatively unexamined status of the child/family nexus in liberal proposals for rationing unequal opportunities for inequality. This is because it is children who become individuals and individuals who give birth to children whose families (however constituted) in turn individualize them. We speak in this way in order not to separate the child from the intragenerational and intergenerational dynamics that frame the child's life opportunities and risks. This is a necessary twist of speech if we are to grasp the idea that child 'risk' is encountered in the very concept of 'opportunity' as defined in liberal ideology. Thus, it belongs to the liberal credo that

1 children are *not visibly predictable* winners/losers in the inequality game;
2 children are *procedurally equal* in any process of talent discrimination; and
3 no child is a predictable winner or loser as a result of the cumulative class effects of competition.

Fairness to children, then, means that they are not to seem to have been born with an unequal chance in the competition that reproduces liberal inequality. But this means that *children's equality* before the law, in the health system, in the education system, and in the employment system is determined by *family inequality* in those systems (Glendon 1989). Nevertheless, these subsystems must themselves appear to deal with children without regard for any other determining factor than need (in the case of health) or merit (in the case of education and employment). The legitimacy of liberal society requires the belief among its individual members that their lives began with a childhood whose ideal circumstances afforded their future prospects. The legacy of such a childhood then enters into the next generation's account of its life-story. Since it is children who at birth are marked by sex, race, and family-background characteristics that are due to no competitive effort of their own, it must be understood that *no pre-social state of nature favours children*. Indeed, children are even more condemned by contractarianism than are their parents, whose individualizing ideologies they have not yet acquired but must be presumed to develop.

The Politics of Child Needs

Only by overlooking the child/family bond can we declare the child's political equality. *Child equality is a myth to which liberalism is committed in order to 'save' the inequality within and between families.* Here, therefore, liberal society stands in need of the recognition that the state must ensure that families not constitute a recognizable impediment to the child's citizenship. The latter notion implies, of course, provision for adult socialization and the learning of such rights and duties that currently constitute their passage from childhood to adulthood (Blustein 1982). Conversely, the state's interest in the child's education, broadly conceived, will involve the state in the prevention of neglect, harm, and abuse to children, even though in liberal ideology the family system ought to escape governance on the grounds that the family is a sphere of privacy or of intimacy without 'other-regarding' concerns. Only a child who can presume upon enormous parental privilege could act as though its life chances represented a set of negotiable claims upon society. In reality, all children require civic assurance of their unconditional presence. This requirement is, however, set to nothing in the liberal definition of the child as potential human capital from whom a dividend may be expected – or, if not, from whom investment may be withdrawn. Such a concept violates the child's civic passage from infancy to youth, endowed by civic institutions that nurture talent and are watchful that no child goes missing, that no child drops out, that no child goes sick or hungry in response to the perception that it is unpromising and unwanted.

It may now be argued that on the social policy and research level what must be exposed in the liberal contractarian theory of child care is that it is grounded in the 'speechlessness' (*infans*, not speaking) of the child. Let us call this the *politics of mutism* – by which we mean that the child's interests are articulated on its behalf by those upon whom it is dependent for achieving its shift from fetal state to relative independence. Thus, the child's experience of justice and care is determined by its unequal relations with adults and elder children – and of course, professional care-managers – without whom it is unlikely to survive.

The political issue of *child mutism* is especially acute, since the articulation of child needs/rights/duties involves a complex discursive and institutional exercise around what is an essentially contested conceptual domain in which there compete

1 expert discourses upon child need/welfare;
2 recipient ('client') counter-discourses upon child need/ welfare; and
3 reprivatization discourses upon child need/welfare.

But while the fate of children and families at risk gives rise to what appears to be an ever-expanding plurality of discourses, in fact liberal society is increasingly dualist. It is, therefore, reasonable to constrain the apparent babel of tongues to the contrastive paradigms of contract and covenant discourses as the organizing languages in the current social-policy debates. For example, if we take the need for 'day care,' it is sensible to ask in whose interests the discourse of 'responsible' day care is articulated:

1 Is it for children?
2 Is it for 'working' mothers?
3 Is it for employers?
4 Is it for society?

Complex arguments circulate around the difference between 'child care' and 'day care,' between licensed and non-licensed day-care operations, between focusing upon child poverty or upon women's poverty. Overall, social policy must eventually decide between targeted programs and a universal system of child care that recognizes the civic function of family and parental care (Powell 1992). We cannot define 'responsible' day care in terms of children's needs without taking into account the ecology of family, economy, and community, from which there derive further interpretative discourses upon what is entailed in the 'need' for day care. It is also clear from the day-care example that a 'need' that might be considered 'private' may be declared 'public' and/or 'reprivatized,' depending upon the prevailing politics of need interpretation (Fraser 1989: 144–90). From the standpoint of the child it may be argued that such concepts as '*day* care,' 'single parent', or 'single-parent family' are biased towards the ideological interests of individualizing adults, especially bourgeois feminists who render the stakes too high for all those women who lack the resources to be competent by the standard of the 'market family' touted by the double-income person/pair.

The Risky Matrix

The other side of how children are spoken for in the politics of the contemporary family is how families headed by single mothers are spoken for by bourgeois feminists who enjoy the privileges of the bourgeois family, selling off its burdens (buying the labour and the infants of single mothers) and doubling their own fortunes in the symbolic capitals of law, business, government, and university. The apologists of late capitalism promote the emancipation of women as producers and consumers by according to them the right to control their own bodies – aborting not only the foetus but all social relationships that limit the myth of postmodernity. Women's bodies become the site of a political struggle between the right and the left in all industrialized societies where *genderless individualism* is envisaged:

> An industrial society cannot exist unless it imposes certain unisex assumptions: the assumptions that both sexes are made for the same work, perceive the same reality, and have, with some minor cosmetic variations, the same needs. And the assumption of scarcity, which is fundamental to economics, is itself logically based on this unisex postulate (Illich 1982: 9–10).

Thus, bourgeois feminists are increasingly committed to individualizing ideologies of

1 sexual freedom;
2 own-body possession and (a) abortion, or (b) keeping the baby; and
3 a family with/without a supporting male/husband.

The consequences of procreative sexuality extended to low-income, low-education, high-minority, high-risk young women are a major source of the risks that attend their birth cohort. It is therefore hopelessly inadequate to include this subculture of young women under middle/upper-class women's culture of sexual freedom, birth-choice, marriage – divorce – remarriage. Rather, the new 'underclass' of single mothers and their offspring are subject to considerable deprivation in the name of class-based sexual life chances that actually render both the 'single life' and the 'married life' scarce achievements for them (McKie 1993).

The younger a child's parent(s), the less stable the conjugal relationship, the lower the parental income, health, and education, and the greater are its own childhood risks from the de-skilling of its parent(s). Such *risky childhoods* are, however, endemic to the liberal inegalitarian reproduction of underprivileged life chances. These risky futures stand in even greater contrast to the scenarios of sexual play, pro-choice, gene-shopping, and toy-children underwritten by the high-tech medicine and liberal professions to which privileged children are destined as they mature and achieve the socio-economic places reserved for bourgeois families. Single mothers constitute a risky matrix owing to their *socially structured carnal ignorance* (O'Neill 1990) in any of the following areas:

 1 sexual disease
 2 contraception
 3 prenatal care
 4 postnatal care
 5 housework
 6 cooking
 7 shopping
 8 literacy
 9 employment
10 health
11 lifestyle

Thus, we have to consider that just as the de-skilling of labour weakens its position in the market, so the de-skilling of families in favour of the smart products and ideologies that they consume in the market-place weakens family authority. The compound effect of poorly resourced families and competitive schooling is to weaken the covenant between children and parents, as well as between children and their community. Children at risk in single-parent families are the shock troops of the bourgeois ideology of marketized family life. They are caught in the crossfire between the new bourgeois family, whose market position enables it to sell off family commitments, and the working/non-working parent, whose labour no longer earns a family wage without subsidy, moonlighting, and child labour in the service economy.

The betrayal of children by market ideologies is just as evident among moral theorists of child/parent relations, who are loath to limit the alleged universality of ethical norms with what they disparagingly term 'particularistic,' 'sentimental,' or 'differential pull' factors that nevertheless arise precisely from the child's embodied dependence upon its care-givers (Sommers 1986). They argue that, since the parent/child relationship is a fait accompli unasked for by the 'moral patient' (the infant), as well as a 'shock' to its parent, there is no filial duty or debt that can be said to constitute the ground of obligation towards parents – and certainly not towards grandparents by their grown children (Holt 1974). In our view, all 'duty-free' conceptions of the family covenant not only undermine families, they also undermine the wider society upon which they nevertheless rely.

What the civic state defends is the covenant of care within the family and between the child's home and school, set in an environment of other civic institutions that furnish the child's assurance that it will be cherished and fostered in its encounter with adult society. All our institutions should work together to reveal to our children the civic commons they are to enjoy, with the hope that one day they too may become its caretakers. Here the child is the inviolable subject of collective assurances that extend from the family and community to the state. It is this civic assurance that is removed in the liberal concept of the child as one who learns to arrogate to itself claims upon society due to the child as an independent subject

FIGURE 3
More Canadian children living in poverty

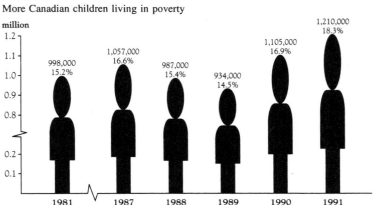

SOURCE: Statistics Canada, *Income Distributions by Size in Canada*, 1991

Poverty is measured using Statistics Canada's Low-income Cut-offs (LICOs), 1986 base. Canada faces the disturbing reality that over 1.2 million children under the age of 18 – almost one in five – live in poverty. Since 1989, the year of the House of Commons resolution to end child poverty, over a quarter of a million children have been added to the ranks of the poor.

of market-based rights enjoyed at the expense of other children who fail to deserve such rewards. The result of the market view of children is clear from figure 3, where one can see that Canada currently tolerates a growing army of children in poverty.

Contractarian society disavows its dependence upon family and kin-community contributions grounded in the life-world covenant that libertarians insist upon treating as prehistorical or pre-political. Covenant theory, by contrast, rejects the ideological subordination of embodied ties and traditions to the disembodied, rational-legal relations of market society. Liberal theorists claim that the covenant order is a primary or primitive institution because it is familized and gendered. This ideological hierarchy of contract over covenant is assumed in all the social sciences (Kohlberg 1984). Its effect upon social policy is to undermine the very order of embodied relationships that social-policy efforts ought to reinforce. In the following chapter, therefore, we shall take up the task of reconceiving the foundations of family and child relations in the double context of sexuality and intergenerationality.

THREE

Reconceiving Family Foundations:
Pro-Creation or Co-Creation?

We must reject the metaphysics of possessive individualism as a basis for sustainable family institutions. We shall do so by reconceiving the grounds of intergenerationality, that is, the continuity of life that extends from the present to the past and from the present to the future of the human family. No one owns the family, no husband owns his wife, no wife owns her husband, no mother owns her child, but all are owned by the gift of life and the cultural legacy that every present generation owes to a previous and future generation. Therefore, intergenerationality cannot be reduced to the possessive practices of the procreative contract and its current sexual ideologies. Moreover, since bourgeois sexuality is ruled by scarcity – because its enjoyment demands that sex be underwritten by contraception and abortion, which are in turn scarcity items – it is necessary to recognize on behalf of children that the covenant of 'co-creation' cannot be reduced to the individualized perspective of the sexual contract. In every child who is conceived we reconceive a future society in which everyone has a stake. The current sexualization of marriage and reproduction that we refer to as the procreative contract is a carrier of the restricted ideology of the present over the past and the future, at the same time that it incurs heavy social costs from weakening the matrix of intergenerationality that is a prime source of civic care.

Family Covenant or Sexual Contract?

Let us trace two paradigms of the foundation of families in order to re-examine our current assumption that the sexual contract is the proper origin of children, who are thereby parental property and committed to the risks and benefits accorded by their family. The covenant paradigm of family and inter-generationality, by contrast, is founded upon a history that is as old as humanity. We call this the family covenant. At the heart of human history we do not find desire, greed, sexuality, power, and profit, except as contemporary fictions of our origins. What we find is the fundamental concern (*Sorge*) that is tended in the worship of the source of human continuity and care from generation to generation, from family to family. By the same token, this worship guarantees to each family its privacy and property in the rites of its ancestors. The covenant family is not founded upon any religious dogma, but on the sociological fact (Durkheim 1912) that what is worshipped by human beings are the ties (*religio*) between them. But these ties are familial and intergenerational before being political or economic. They thoroughly pervade all later political economy until the modern period, which we define by the autonomy of the market and contract-individualism as the dominant institutions over everyday life and its ritual events of birth, marriage, and death.

The *tabula rasa* or clean-slate individual of liberal contract theory is as much a fiction as is its counterpart fiction of the many-headed monster state, or Leviathan. Each device serves to stampede thought into those forced alternatives of the under- or over-socialized individual (Wrong 1962). In reality, nobody enters the world except by means of another body, whose bond with yet another body is the basic social cell of intercorporeality that is presupposed in the birth of any individual (O'Neill 1989). It is only a romantic fiction that marks birth as the appearance of an individual rather than as the reappearance of a family. What is involved here are two time-frames within the life-world. 'Birth' marks both an *intra*-generational event within a 'marriage' and an *inter*-generational event between 'families'. Or we might say that a birth marks the inaugural moment of the 'parents,' in the first case, and of the 'grandparents,' in the second. Once we reconsider the nuclear thinking underlying contractarian social theory in the light of the intercorporeal and intergenerational relations between individuals, we can just as well say that men and women form families in order to have extended families as we can say that individuals form sexual unions in order to have sex. In other words, the procreative interests of individuals are ruled by sexually related but autonomous kinship values that are enjoyed through intergenerationality and not only through the sexual contract. Thus, the trauma of divorce resides in the breaking of family and not only in the breaking of the sexual contract between husband and wife. The loss to society is the loss of a potential intergenerational turn, a failure to transcend the contingencies of two-person love and hatred. For the same reason, the trauma of divorce settlements is due not solely to the renegotiation of a property contract but also to the reduction of the family resources that underwrite intergenerationality.

The indivisibility of the child is the limit of the contract model of family. Indeed, the child can only be inscribed in the contract family through rights discourses that preserve the adult ideology of individualized membership in consensual and revisable contracts. From this standpoint, the child is conceived as the freely chosen by-product of a sexual apparatus (contraception, abortion, gender selection, and DNA-shopping) to render the radically contingent event of birth and parenthood a specifically rational choice of new life. Strictly speaking, human reproduction raises as much of a conundrum for utilitarian individualism as any other altruistic behaviour, unless one has no conception of the other-responsibilities in a pregnancy and birth. A denial of such responsiblities is only possible if we imagine individuals who copulate entirely apart from families. But this is a state of affairs that human society has only ever conceived as a pre-human state, that is, one of animality or barbarism prior to the founding of human families, whose reproduction enters us into history and kinship. Thus, all violations of human order are likened to copulation outside of kinship – however much such violations may have been the pastime of the gods and goddesses of mythology.

The most sacred principle in the founding of human institutions is the covenant principle that the family is the passage from one family to another, from age to age (Lévi-Strauss 1969; Freud 1913). Violations of this covenant are violations of intergenerationality over and above the individual injury in sexual seduction. All other crimes derive their repulsiveness from the degree to which they similarly incapacitate social exchange – whatever their harm to persons and property. By contrast, much of what we call religious, moral, and ethical behaviour is involved in our respect for the life in others who are in turn bearers of the life of others. Such a covenant exceeds the sciences of sociology, psychology, economics, and politics because it furnishes the pre-contractual ground of all our contracts. *There is nothing metaphysical about the family covenant.* If it exceeds us, it does so only as the life-world in which we all dwell and which none of us thinks of exhausting by any scheme with which we may overlap it; for it has always endured these things, renewing itself with our prayers.

Families were first founded to bury their dead. The dead were buried in order to remain close to their families. The tombs of Greece and Rome had a cooking-place where meals could be offered to the dead souls who continued to live in the grave. The care of their dead, therefore, was the basic duty of every family. This meant that in every home there was an altar upon which a fire was always kept alive. The life of the fire was the life of the family's generations. Everything cooked upon the family hearth was shared between past and present generations. The significance of the family fire was not sexual, Freud notwithstanding. It was the principle of moral order; in other words, the guardian of the reproductive cycle in nature and in the family, each observant of the other. Thus, we may say either that the most ancient religions were domestic or that the most ancient families were religious; that is, that each was the foundation of the other, observing the mystery of generation that each family worshipped according to its own private rites, passed down from father to son in patrimony:

> This religion could be propagated only by generation. The father, in giving life to his son, gave him at the same time his creed, his worship, the right to continue the sacred fire, to offer the funeral meal, to pronounce the formulas of prayer. Generation established a mysterious bond between infant, who was born to life, and all the gods of the family – θεοί σύναιμοι were of his blood – θεοί εγγενείς. The child, therefore, received at his birth the right to adore them, and to offer them sacrifices; and later, when death should have deified him, he also would be counted, in his turn, among the gods of the family. (De Coulanges 1901: 47)

The foundation of a family lay in its *intergenerational piety* rather than in its marital contract. The purpose of a marriage was not to keep love alive but to prevent the extinction of the rites owed to the family line. Thus, neither the male nor the female belonged to themselves but only to the family line in which they worshipped. By the same token, what made families private was not the intimacy of the conjugal union but the enclosure (*Penates*) within which the sacred rites of the family were practised. Property was private because the grave was private and could not be confounded with another. 'Religion, and not laws, first guaranteed the right of property.' However, this meant that it was the domestic gods and not the living, labouring individual who had rights over the land:

> It is not the individual actually living who has established his right over this soil, it is the domestic god. The individual has it in trust only; it belongs to those who are dead, and to those who are yet to be born. It is part of the body of this family, and cannot be separated from it. (Ibid.: 91).

The ancient family did not even belong to itself, as we think of it in terms of modern notions of privacy and procreative contract. Having originated only in sacred memory, it could not be possessed by its contemporary members. It could not be bought or sold. It could only be preserved or extinguished. Strictly speaking, then, nothing could be inherited in such a family except the duty to practise its worship:

> To form an idea of inheritance among the ancients, we must not figure to ourselves a fortune which passes from the hands of one to another. The fortune is immovable, like the hearth, and the tomb to which it is attached. It is the man who passes away. It is the man who, as the family unrolls its generations, arrives at his hour appointed to continue the worship, and to take care of the domain. (Ibid.: 95).

We have set forth a genealogy of the covenant concept of family foundation because it is fast becoming a shibboleth of social reporting that 'the family' no longer exists. What is actually contested is that a secular variant of the family, that is, a married couple with two children and a single wage, should any longer be the political norm (McKie 1993). Whether or not this political stance serves to reduce the stigmatization of broken families, it is essential not to produce a reverse stigmatism with the implication that the heterosexual family life works against democracy. No family is 'the family,' since the idea of family as an institution founded upon the absolute value of intergenerationality can only be honoured in principle. At the same time, the intergenerational family may serve as a regulative notion in the derivation of social policies whose task is to sustain families in difficulties of one kind or another but for which we need some benchmark of viability.

The New Foundlings

It is important not to speak of 'poor families' when what we mean is that without sufficient resources it is hard to sustain family life, kinship, and community (Keating and Mustard 1993). To make this point clear, we have given considerable attention to single-parent family life, because we consider it poorly served for the prevention of risk to itself and to its children. Children who are born to young women who remain mothers but whose fathers do not remain husbands are born into families whose authority can only be sustained through state provision. From the moment of conception these children are exposed to the risks of contract sexuality rather than received into a communal covenant of intergenerationality. Yet we shall argue that these two notions of family foundation cannot be isolated. It is only on an extremely narrow understanding of 'procreation' that the implicit institutional concerns inscribed in the term *pro-* (on behalf of) *creation* can be ignored in favour of its biological sense as sexual reproduction, any more than we should ignore the institutional trace contained in the word *re-* (again) production. If we lose sight of the distinction between the responsibility for life and the reproduction of life, we lose the civic assurance that goes with childhood as intergenerational passage through family life. We lose the thickness of intergenerational relationships between parents and children within the fold of grandparent and grandchild relations. We lose the spatio-temporal expansion of childhood, family, and community in the narrow confines of single-parent poverty.

Today, it is quite impossible to assume without debate that child/parent relationships are ruled by the life-world practices of kin/community, since the latter are also increasingly delegiti-mated by the professional/legal and medical/therapeutic agencies that intervene between child and parent inside and outside of the welfare state (O'Neill and Ruddick 1979). Thus, the question of what constitutes 'opportunity' or 'risk' in respect of 'children' can only be addressed with respect to the competing claims of those having the authority to produce the treatments, laws, and practices that in the home, school, hospital, workplace, and street determine family life chances, risks, and benefits. Under these circumstances, the life chances of children must be looked at in terms of an ecological approach (Bronfenbrenner 1979; Glossop 1988) to the changes in family/household structures and their resourcefulness in adapting to changes in the level and structure of employment and underemployment (Shields 1993). Broadly speaking, the following features are to be observed:

1 an increase in single person or couple households (surviving elders, divorced singles)
2 a decline in intergenerational households
3 an increase in female-headed households
4 an increase of married women in the labour force
5 a decline in employment for young people

Thus, single-mother households with growing children have suffered a decline in per capita resources, aggravated by their lack of kin networks, although some are able to count upon their elders for help. In other households, elders without chil-dren or with few children experience dependency either with-out caretakers or with severely reduced care owing to the time demands on a working mother/daughter. Children are caught in the middle – often destined for long periods of unemploy-ment in and out of school, while their parents cope with a similar syndrome, squeezing their own children.

Here we encounter another family paradox, namely, that the provision of welfare by the state is even more fragmented by the relative strength of a family, that is, its residential stability, reciprocity networks, the number and age of members able to find some sort of employment or retraining. In the same context, however, we find a *collapse of intergenerationality*, inasmuch as members of the same family may be in competition for work or unemployment benefits:

> Certain households are becoming increasingly more fortunate, whereas others are becoming increasingly more deprived. Thus, to put it positively, some – but certainly not all – households with 'core' workers and other members of the households also in employment (either full or part-time) are able to achieve and to maintain high household incomes and substantial affluence, despite the individually weak labour market position of some of their members. (Pahl 1988: 251)

As a result of the preceding trends, three out of five children at risk in 1991 are children born into another youth's poverty (see figure 4), or into the *single-parent poverty syndrome.* These are Canada's new foundlings, whose plight renders ever more urgent the task of rethinking family and child care.

A complex ideological matrix currently shapes child/society relations, so that we cannot simply play off covenant institutions of primary care against contract institutions of secondary-care. Rather, we must start from a structural paradox of risk in family and institutional care, that is, the recognition that, contrary to the liberal fiction of individualized life-chances, a child's start in life is only intelligible in terms of its family's circumstances, inasmuch as these relay

1 bio-risks incurred in the uterine environment;
2 bio-psychic and socio-psychological risks incurred in the domestic environment;
3 socio-economic risks incurred in the social class environment of the family;
4 global risks incurred by families and communities.

FIGURE 4
Child poverty rates by family type

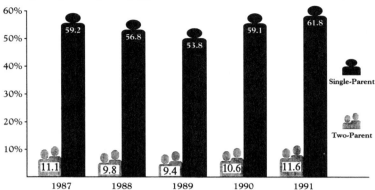

SOURCE: Calculations provided by the Centre for International Statistics, using Statistics Canada's Survey of Consumer Finances microdata files

This complex structure of risk determines to different degrees the vulnerability of children born into families whose class and national *comparative (dis)advantages* make it obvious that 'risk-reduction' can only be undertaken jointly by kin/community and welfare-state agencies engaged in the reduction of illness, ignorance, abuse, and unemployment.

Child Rights versus Child Covenant

> Clearly, the view that contractual relations are a model for human relations generally is especially unsuitable for considering the relations between mothering persons and children. It stretches credulity even further than most philosophers can tolerate to imagine babies as little rational calculators contracting with their mothers for care. (Held 1987: 120)

The metaphysics of liberal individualism is particularly problematic when it comes to our understanding of the fundamental grounds of family relationships (Daniels 1988) and the practice of welfare intervention. Metaphysical individualism requires that the child and the parent each be distinct entities that may 'as such' enter into relationships of contract, rights, and duties (Franklin 1986). Thus, in order to save the sexual-contract theory of family – and its neglect of the embodied covenant involved between child and parent – many are currently engaged in the production of individualizing discourses based upon bio-medical, legal, and socio-psychological arguments directed to

Life-stages		*Family relations*
1 the embryo		1 mother
2 the infant	AND	2 father
3 the child		3 surrogate mother
4 the youth		4 adoptive family

Here, of course, we currently envision the bio-technological future of the extra-familial egg as the ultimate body part that will complete the marketization of the family. Although the Age of Abortion is inaugurated for political and sentimental reasons, its future lies in the market-place, where a bio-proletariat will supply body parts and fetal by-products – of which the latest are 'designer babies' and 'retirement pregnancies.' Here market mothers are served at the price of the extinction of a fetal mother to produce babies whose intergenerational history has been erased. Out of these complex relations (Arditti 1989; Grobstein 1988; Cohen 1990), we can expect to see the continuing production of socio-legal discourses that divide between

a. children's rights and
b. family rights.

The two systems of rights are unlikely to be mutually coherent. Currently, there are attempts (Holt 1974; Franklin 1986) to define children's rights on the liberal model of individual rights exercised by potentially autonomous agents – despite the reality of children's dependency. Thus, the necessity of recognizing parent/guardian's rights/duties means that family rights cannot be wholly reduced either to women's or to children's rights:

> To distinguish parental discipline from abuse, and consenting sex from sexual assualt, is to make a social, not simply a private choice. It is to acknowledge that human rights are social products, and that civil society transcends the contest between government and individual, labour union and corporation, husband and wife. Here, the nature of human rights is determined communicatively, through debate aimed at comprehension, including awareness of ethnic, cultural and sexual difference. The purpose is to do more than identify individual rights as they are: it is to contextualize them in light of their prospective social benefits and effects. It is to shift them from a narrow liberal conversation to a multifaceted and human context within a participatory democracy. (Trakman 1991: 1–2)

A fully fledged child-rights system would require, to be consistent with the metaphysics of the sexual contract, that the respective utilities of the child or parent be counted of equal worth and that the two parties – separate and equal – confront each other in an adversarial mode to settle contracts. By contrast, the family-rights system would need to be grounded in the embodied family covenant – whose history we have sketched earlier – and whose elements are the constitutive relationships that hold between

1 courtship and commitment;
2 commitment and copulation;
3 copulation and conception;

4 conception and birth;
5 birth and infancy;
6 child and parental care;
7 grandchild and grandparent care; and
8 family and community care.

From the covenant perspective, 'pro-choice' discourse represents an extreme ideological attachment to the metaphysics of possessive individualism, despite the socio-legal framework that delimits such possessiveness, given the contrary facts of

a. the public-health requirements for copulation;
b. the socio-legal nature of the womb;
c. the ethico-legal nature of the embryo;
d. the socio-legal nature of marriage and family.

> Judges who opt out of the social life of pregnant women as a *genus*, assume that they have no obligation towards the *genus*, only towards the individual ... They disregard the observation that pregnancy, instead of being an isolated state, is a communal condition that embraces groups in which individuals, including pregnant women, participate. (Trakman 1991: 188)

Progenitors, so far from being 'owners' of ovum, sperm, and womb, should rather be considered *trustees* of Life, whose embodied cycle is repeated in their own case with some understanding that this trust is to be exercised in a way conformable with cultural rearing practices that are everywhere understood by and community (Blustein 1982). We currently run the risk of allowing women to reject maternity by themselves or to confer paternity by their same will inasmuch as they choose insemination. Whereas the metaphysics of trust are both universal and historical, current 'pro-choice' ideology represents a one-sided privileging of the grammar of *bio-parenthood* over the grammar of *cultural parenthood*, quite apart from its sexist limitations vis-à-vis fathers and its ageist exclusion of grandparents. Rather, from the cultural perspective of family covenants 'both' parents have children, while recognizing that one or other – or both where day care is involved – may not have the major role in their care, supposing the state sustains our general concern for child care.

In view of the internal relationships that constitute parenthood, it may be useful to consider Sibyl Schwarzenbach's argument for the recognition of reproduction as an alternative model of 'making' in contrast with the craft model of labour, which in turn underlies bourgeois-feminist possessive individualism and what we have called the politics of child mutism. Here, again, we have two grammars of care. The distinctive work of mothering (which should involve both parents) involves a communicative relationship that is non-possessive but responsible. It is marked by stewardship and is, above all, a gift relation:

> The alternative model of 'making something one's own' presented here is one which by definition cannot be exclusive and private. Such 'owning' may be considered an appropriation, not of the natural physical world, but of the 'human social' one. It implies that in an important sense we in fact do make other people 'our own', although this form must now be carefully distinguished from traditional ownership as a control or 'domination' of them. On the contrary, this form essentially entails a responsiveness to concrete need, as well as the encouragement of another's autonomous capacities. It thus emphasizes that long neglected aspect of 'ownership' as *in*clusion (participation, '*zu Hausesein*') in the specifically human community. Moreover, the model clearly pre-supposes an altered conception of personality, one which now emphasizes the 'fact of continuity' with others over that of 'separateness.' (Schwarzenbach 1987: 159)

The uterine covenant, in which we are obliged to respect a

certain dispossession in 'having' a child, must be inviolable, even where conception is a matter of choice and whatever the projected satisfactions of the family group (Schoeman 1980). This is because no society considers 'procreation' to be a private indulgence, whatever its stand on copulation. While many believe that *contra*-ception breaks the bond between copulation and conception, very few believe that once copulation has resulted in conception the progenitors are free to abort the embryo without regard to God, state, and family interests in *pro*-creation (Dworkin 1993) that would require a severe ritual of consent in reaching such a decision.

Who Cares?

Sullivan (1992) has carefully explored the difficulties arising from a rights-based approach to the relationships between children, families, and state agencies. Along with Gaylin and Macklin (1982), he sees advantages in an obligation approach towards children recognized as such and not confused with minority groups of one kind and another. Apart from all the troubles of political mutism involved in speaking on behalf of children's rights, as well as the forced alternatives of adult and child status (Minow 1986), the welfare of young children involves larger social relations than those between the child and the courts:

> Given the uncontrolled effects of the law, its value in moderating domination notwithstanding, it behooves us to make concerted and innovative efforts outside the law to advance the position of young persons within the family and the human community. In this project, the current crisis in public spending, real or ideological, will provide some tactical opportunities to advance vernacular community approaches. (Sullivan 1992: 160)

The current conflict between child and family ideologies

mediated by professionals ignores the equal vulnerability of parents and children (Mohr 1984). A community-based approach might be more responsive to the issues involved. While strengthening the politics of childhood, the community approach nevertheless stands in competition with the more powerful courts, hospitals, and police, unless we can bring about some re-allocation of social resources in this regard. However, to the extent that we can move to a more convivial model of local justice, children and communities are likely to benefit from a covenant rather than contractarian concept of social justice.

The issue of 'who cares?' is further aggravated when the family is cut off from its extended kin and community. In these circumstances, all of us, including non-parental adults, have a role to play in the work of intergenerational care and trust that must pervade the lives of children. Parents, grandparents, and local figures in the community should all be involved in child care so that our concern for children is not reduced to the private anxieties of possessive families and their demands upon professional care, from which so many children will be excluded. However we look at it, the care of children as well as of sick and older people remains largely the work of women (Finch and Groves 1983; Finch 1989). This is especially so in the practice of hands-on care, whether provided in kin/community settings or in professional medicalized-care systems. The same is true of 'day' care. While men as well as women work in both care systems, wherever women have professional qualifications they will be less likely to perform hands-on care functions than their less-qualified sisters and brothers. Similarly, 'executive women' may employ immigrant women for day care – even at below the legal minimum wage – while other working women make use of women relatives and improvised day-care services when care facilities are not provided by their employers. Likewise, in Canada a legal 'Ms.' with a joint family income of $100,000 or more does not hesitate to claim disadvantage, inasmuch as for tax purposes she makes a day-care deduction of $13,000 a year – rather than the (then) allowable $2000 that any other working-class woman might have made. In both cases, however, child care is treated as a market cost paid to another woman whose own market position is unlikely to allow a similar expense and deduction. Thus, the care function is not 'natural' to women in two cases – each of which is ordinarily taken to be the opposite of the other:

1 Where it is a *gendered* task like other tasks exercised by males or females in the society.
2 Where it is a function of the *femalization* of tasks in an industrialized society.

In either case, it is culture not nature that defines care as a woman's task. But whereas in a gendered economy (Illich 1982; Wilson 1989) the social division of labour between males and females is *different but not unequal*, it is only in an industrialized economy that we can speak of the *inequality of occupations that are similar*. In an industrial society women's work is not 'natural' to females because of their sex; it is sexist because of the 'natural' inequality that defines all occupations in an industrial society.

To argue 'equal pay for equal work' might correct sexism *within* occupations but it does not alter income inequality *between* occupations. This is the fundamental source of class inequality for men, women, and children alike. Thus, an executive woman who earns $500,000 a year, while paying a day-care worker about $12,000 a year, hardly conceives of paying the working woman more than the 'going rate' for day-care or domestic work. This point is made because it is important not to confuse the two grammars of work. Wherever care is shifted into the market economy, it is *paid but poorly paid work* and, like other low-income service jobs, open to the least skilled workers. By contrast, for as long as care remains in the gendered economy of kin/community services, it is *work but not a job*, and the grammar of pay, inequality, and feminization on these issues does not rule in the care-provider's self-concept, because it is fulfilled in a gift relation (Mauss 1967) that it would be entirely incongruous to imagine in contractarian terms:

> One might think of the gift relationship as a kind of politics: like the vote, the petition, and the demonstration, the gift is a way of giving concrete meaning to the union of citizens. And as welfare generally aims at overcoming the dominance of money in the sphere of need, so the active participation of citizens in the business of welfare (and security, too) aims at making sure that the dominance of money is not simply replaced by the dominance of political power. (Walzer 1983: 94)

Children, of course, have an interest in being cared for – whether by kin or by an agency of the state. Child welfare in this respect is heavily dependent upon men and women at work in the home and in community services. In terms of the distinction we have drawn between the two grammars of work, there is much to be gained for families from the recognition of social care as civic work, without identifying its recognition uniquely with compensation as the mark of 'real work.' Paid work is exploited, unpleasant, and demeaning in the great part, except where persons derive their self-worth elsewhere – that is, from their families and communities. The point about the claims of citizenship in welfare states is that self-respect must be maintained independently of employment/unemployment, age, sex, or race, whereas the market generates respect for some at the risk of disrespect for most. In this regard, uncompensated civic work remains a huge factor in the generation of self-worth and community respect for *both* men and women. Since children also derive their self-respect and autonomy from their families, they too have an enormous stake in the citizenship principle of respect for persons guaranteed by the welfare state. In the context of deindustrialization, it becomes essential for the state to underwrite recognition and respect for workers in any sector of the economy, however limited, as well for those who contribute to the services of the civic economy.

We are in danger of producing a care-intensive society by way of destroying the covenant of care in non-commoditized exchanges between family members and community institutions. Professional 'care-takers' now proliferate in a society that – like the denizens of apartment buildings – has no time to care for itself. The potential degradation of gendered care constitutes a serious threat to the public voice of families as well as children. It also erases the distinctively moral voice of care (Gilligan 1982) in the politics of the family, whereas caring deserves equal place with justice claims in our civic discourse. In our view, men and women have always given their time to community-care activities even if it has been along gendered lines, and both are deprived by any ideology that claims care concern is more primitive than justice concern – or more private than public. Both perspectives are complementary dimensions of ethical concern. The differential socialization of children and the role-specific values learned in primary and secondary institutions combine to impose upon both males and females a social division that both males and females have had to learn to soften according to their civic circumstance. By the same token, our map of moral development (Inhelder and Piaget 1958; Kholberg 1984) must be redrawn in a less unilinear and homogenizing fashion in order to take on the crucial issue of how children themselves will in future learn a caring ethic in a world where the adults, male and female, are increasingly surrendered to the abstract, formal justice ethic. In the meantime, however, our educational curriculum is largely predicated on developmental theories (Inhelder and Piaget 1958) and grading practices that represent separation, individuation, and autonomy as the goals of maturation, despite the way these create deficits in the civic and altruistic conduct of everyday life.

Anyone concerned with the development of children into future citizens must be concerned to readdress the split between attachment values and autonomy values that characterizes their shift from childhood to adulthood as it is currently coded for market futures:

> The different parameters of the parent-child relationship – its inequality and its interdependence or attachment – may ground different feelings which differentiate the dimensions of inequality/equality and attachment/detachment that characterize all forms of human connection. In contrast to a unitary moral vision and to the assumption that the opposite of the one is the many, these two dimensions of relationship provide coordinates for reimagining the self and remapping development. The two conceptions of responsibility, reflecting different images of the self in relationship, correct an individualism that has been centred within a single interpretative framework. (Gilligan 1988: 5)

It is now argued among some feminist political theorists (Elshtain 1990b; Held 1987; Schwarzenbach 1987) that, in view of the necessity to delimit the abstract generalization of the contract paradigm in social and political life, we need to think of the family and the household as a potential model (which we call the covenant paradigm) for a new polity and civility. Such a move might reduce the excessive rationalism, possessiveness, and aggression that rule in the male political arena:

> Instead of importing into the household principles derived from the marketplace, perhaps we should export to the wider society the relations suitable for mothering persons and children. This

approach suggests that just as relations between persons within the family should be based on concern and caring, rather then on egoistic or non-tuistic contracts, so various relations in the wider society should be characterized by more care and concern and openness and trust and human feeling than are the contractual bargains that have developed so far in political and economic life, or even than are aspired to in contractarian prescriptions. Then, the household instead of the marketplace might provide a model for society. (Held 1987: 122)

From our perspective, we cannot refashion family values without reducing the class divisions between families. It is essential to civic sustainability that we adopt a positive stance on the renewal of welfare-state agency in order to revivify kin-community care, to reverse the de-skilling of families, and to complement their civic care-capacity with professional agencies that are not solely devoted to the repair of failures in health, education, and employment. By the same token, we do not mean to familize social care but to extend the social covenant to agents who are *anyone* and *everyone*. Thus, on the complementary level of collective reciprocity, what is needed is the political will to reconstruct the welfare state so that it is neither an ersatz family nor simply a therapeutic repair-shop for the failures of market society. We reject any idea of the welfare state as a colony for those whose family misfortunes render them vulnerable to exclusion by market forces whose indifference to civic sustainability is the principal abuse in our polity.

We recognize that the wider society is too complex to be governed by even a revised model of the caring family, because family conduct is continuously reshaped by the wider society of civic concern. In the following chapter we return to the larger concept of the covenant of care, which (as we shall see in chapter 5) is itself shaped by definite rules of reciprocity that must operate both within and between generations.

FOUR

The Covenant of Care

In liberal theory society is regarded as the necessary background to the market, whereas the state is considered an unnecessary interference. In practice, however, the market undermines liberal society because it breaks its moral bonds but then turns to the state to protect it against crime and rebellion inspired by the very inequality and injustice that derive from the market. Inasmuch as liberalism still seeks to delimit the excesses of the market, it yearns for a return to the moral foundations of civil society. This is the source of liberal conservatism. Thus, liberalism also holds to a concept of limited government, but it is unable to give either to society or to the state the trust and solidarity that would renew civility. The liberal concept of civil society lacks any roots in history, in sentiment, and in reciprocity, whose authority we locate in the practices of civic sustainability that derive from community and state provision. Liberal voluntarism expresses itself through gratuity rather than reciprocity. It offers charity to others in the name of a selflessness that is not beholden to those who are to receive its offer. But reciprocity is due to unavoidable presence, history, and embodiment that is neither selfish nor selfless. The covenant of reciprocity cries out against the charitable laundering of selfishness as selflessness.

Civic society must avoid the twin errors of liberalism,

namely, the false view that we can have society without reciprocity and that we can have an economy without a polity. Civic society, however, is not the creature of the welfare state, anymore than it is independent of market forces. Civic society is, properly speaking, the ground of economy and citizenship. It therefore requires us to reconceive our practice of citizenship in order to rescue it from current political marketeering, from which Canadian citizens recoil. This is quite evident from Canadians' response to any 1993 election tactic of selling off the national consensus around basic social programs. The present essay is, then, a concerted effort to spell out the grammar of the Canadian aspiration to preserve our basic social fabric in what we have called a Civic Covenant. We want to defend the institutions that Canadians enjoy through the endowment and obligations of civic sustainability.

We conceive the covenant of care as a practice that extends civic responsibility from the womb to the streets, from children to elders, from physicians and social workers to single mothers and taxpayers. We do so because we reject the liberal contamination of public space and time by every manner of risk to citizens as much as we reject its counterpart possessive ideology of embodiment, desire, knowledge, and health. We reject the liberal mode of enjoyment practised without regard for the misery and pain of others. We reject the liberal ghetto; we abhor liberal insularity with its lamentable fears of contamination, crime, and disease and its uncivil investment in immunity from self-induced hostilities.

How are we to regard the homeless, the vagrants, the unemployed, the addicts, and the emotionally or mentally impaired people whom we encounter in the streets and before shops, theatres, churches, and cafés? How are we to restrain our fear of them, our disgust, frustration, and resignation? What does it help to give or to refuse beyond imposing upon ourselves an awkward morality that we know is no longer funded by our civic institutions? Nothing so alters the course of our day, nothing so degrades our own small affairs and their minor pleasures as does the encounter with persons whose look we shun, whose existence we deny while requiring of them peaceful recognition of ourselves. Under such conditions, who is wealthy?

Today, we increasingly celebrate trust between persons, if not equality and charity, while destroying trust between classes, races, sexes, and generations. Thus, we strain to privatize our ethics, while hoping that our public morality can be funded by the welfare state or by rights legislation that will handle those residual but ineradicable contingencies ·which render others vulnerable to the permanent deprivations in such a society. In the hope of ghettoizing our public troubles, we neuroticize our private ethics, always fearful that the wall between our own manageable lives and the despair of those who cannot manage will collapse. Under such conditions, who can be healthy?

We think Canadians regard the state as an institutional expression of the social commons, where citizenship is an exercise of membership that can neither be acquired nor lost like a thing in the market-place. The civic state we have in mind is not merely a no-risk environment; nor is it a 'safety net' extended to shelter citizens from the harshness of the market. It is a repository of affirmed responsibilities and contributions that must be regenerated through civic practice and example. It calls for sacrifice in the same sense that a child calls for its parent's sacrifice, that is, as an unconditional gift in which both are enriched while each is indebted to that intergenerational transmission through which they take their own turn upon the civic stage. Liberal social theory claims to enlighten us with its talk of individualism, equality, progress, and environmental improvement. But families and communities each need roots that will hold against what the harsh market economy of success/failure has in store for them. As we have seen earlier, liberal individualism unleashes selfishness without regard for place or past, and at whatever cost. In the face of these forces, a covenant regard for institutions espouses the daily necessities that in the life of communities, families and children constitute the everyday goodness of their lives.

Security is the civic foundation of everything else that may wondrously supervene upon family and children routines. Among children, reasonableness is the incarnate practice of an understanding that breeds in the bodily presences of their elders and siblings. It is not a contract or a bargain. A child's intelligence is woven into the traditions of its family's senses, manners, and reason, which are its shaping surround. A child is itself and its circumstance. It is from a child's embodied circumstance that things and others around it have the ancestral shape of need, of friend and family, of use and advice. It is from these common things that a child takes on its moods like the changing light of day, acquires its resignation, its hope, and its brooding memory at the same time as it is witness to plain talk, vice, and unfulfilled virtue. A child is all these things day in and day out; and what we offer any child in the midst of these things is that child's very light and our own reflection; and what it holds out to us is our own gift. A child's family and its social circumstance (its neighbours, shopkeepers, teachers, policemen) are the child's legacy of sense and reason, of self and thing, self and other. This surrounding circumstance of kin and community is in turn a work of love and not a possession. It is not inherited because it cannot be owned. It is received in trust by all who are party to it and passed on as long as the generations of our kind endure. Within this covenant no one should seek privilege and exception except as gifts to be shared with others in the celebration of that particular family and community that welcomes our birth, prevents our injury, and mourns our death:

> And thus, too, these families, not otherwise than with every
> family in the earth, how each, apart, how inconceivably lonely,

sorrowful, and remote! Not one other on earth, nor in any dream, that can care so much what comes to them, so that even as they sit at the lamp and eat their supper, the joke they are laughing at could not be so funny to anyone else; and the littlest child who stands on the bench solemnly, with food glittering all over his cheeks in the lamplight, this littlest child I speak of is not there, he is of another family, and it is a different woman who wipes the food from his cheeks and takes his weight upon her thighs and against her body and who feeds him, and lets his weight slacken against her in his heavying sleep; and the man who puts another soaked cloth to the skin cancer on his shoulder; it is his wife who is looking on, and his child who lies sunken along the floor with his soft mouth broad open and his nakedness up like a rolling dog, asleep: and the people next up the road cannot care in the same way, not for any of it: for they are absorbed upon themselves ... All over the whole round earth and in the settlements, the towns, and the great iron stones of cities, people are drawn inward within their little shells of rooms, and are to be seen in their wondrous and pitiful actions through the surfaces of their lighted windows by thousands, by millions, little golden aquariums, in chairs, reading, setting tables, sewing, playing cards, not talking, talking, laughing inaudibly, mixing drinks, at radio dials, eating, in shirt sleeves, carefully dressed, courting, teasing, loving, seducing, undressing, leaving the room empty in its empty light, alone and writing a letter urgently, in couples married, in separate chairs, in family parties, in gay parties, preparing for bed, preparing for sleep: and none can care, beyond that room; and none can be cared for, by any beyond that room: and it is small wonder they are drawn together so cowardly close, and small wonder in what dry agony of despair a mother may fasten her talons and her vampire mouth upon the soul of her struggling son and drain him empty, light as a locust shell: and wonder only that an age that has borne its children and must lose and has lost them, and lost life, can bear further living; but so it is. (Agee and Evans 1966: 51–2)

In contrast with this great corporeal tradition of intergenerationality, liberal anthropology is prospective. It gambles upon
refashioning destinies. It ignores the bonds of birth and family,
the connections of blood and the inevitability of death. Liberal
contracts espouse the future on behalf of a retrospective dis-
covery of opportunity in the chances of birth, family, class,
and neighbourhood. The bond of covenant, by contrast, weds
institutions to family time. It respects surfaces beneath which
there lies a silent corporeality in our lives that is the legacy of
this body and this family of ours. It is beholden to the mutual
work of our senses and intellect that enables us to touch others
and to take from them some kind of knowing whose offer can
never be refused and that we must always venture from our
side.

Covenant destinies are entirely removed from the jackpot
futures that are the fancy of the market-place. The lifestyle of
the rich who are famous only for being rich demands recognition for its ability to plunder those places in the world whose
wealth is in their beauty, serenity, and value grounded in that
civility whose lack is the poverty of the rich. At the same
time, the endless search by the rich for a serenity whose civic
provision at home they deplete demands a culture of prisons
and police that drains the state purse and diverts its attention
from the cause of social justice. But the best strategy for civic
health and security is the care of the commons that nurtures
the talent and the good life to be found anywhere in local
schools, theatres, arenas, streets, shops, and places of worship
that the jackpot, superstar system pillages but cannot provision. This is because talent is nurtured in the institutions of
collective performance, which achievement would be degraded
by the imposition of failure and docility that occurs in the
success system adored in the market-place.

Covenant care is therefore governed by its profound respect
for the particulars of place, time, and conduct from which we
build our civic institutions and form the reciprocities of trust

that sustain our public lives. Covenant practice seeks to devise social policies that remain faithful to the original openness through which our civic concern for others first enters into their lives. Within this covenant we strive never to remove ourselves from the mutual regard that shapes our joys, our sorrows, and our hopes for every human undertaking, whether it is the building of a bridge or the birth of a child. Covenant theory entails a practice of care and concern in the commerce of our daily talk, lookings, helpings, hurts, and angers. By the same token, it celebrates the rituals of our shared lives, of our own growth, and the place others have in our lives, without which we should be diminished and lonely. As Northrop Frye remarks:

> It is becoming apparent that concern is a normal dimension of everybody, including scholars, and that for scholars in particular it is the corrective to detachment, and prevents detachment from degenerating into indifference ... It seems obvious that concern has nothing directly to do with the content of knowledge, but that it establishes the human context into which the knowledge fits, and to that extent informs it. The language of concern is the language of myth, the total vision of the human situation, human destiny, human aspirations and fears. (Frye 1976: 16)

Covenant and Code in Medical Care

In the practice of the social professions we are called upon to fathom the depths of human injury and the intersensory and ancestral connections of mankind, whose infinitude has an awesome ability to absorb injustice, beauty, rage, horror, and frivolity. The practice of care and concern upon which our social life is founded is, properly speaking, a covenant of both sentiment and science that is manifested as much in help to the poor as in manipulating Keynesian variables to stabilize the modern economy. Social care and the reduction of public risk belongs to this covenant of civilized sentiment and knowledge.

How covenant theory interprets social care may be seen if we consider the contrast between the code and the covenant in contemporary professional medicine (May 1975). Thus, the Hippocratic oath contains two sets of obligations:

a. an ethical *code* governing the doctor's treatment of patients;

b. a *covenant* governing the doctor's relation to the teacher and the teacher's progeny, enjoining the teacher to transmit medical knowledge without fee to anyone who takes the Hippocratic oath.

Like all professional codes of care and service, the medical code tends to stylize itself, to become indifferent to both the practitioner and patient/client (physicians become just as driven as their stressed patients), and ultimately to become confined to the moment of treatment. The medical code does not shape the future; it merely outlives those who practise it from day to day. By contrast, the physician's covenant is an intergenerational moment consecrated through a historical gift of teaching: it rests upon a promise of reciprocity flowing from this gift and the determination of all future life in the light of that historic moment of the first gift of membership in the covenant of healing. But in narrowly professionalized practice the covenant is separated from its code, with the result that the most general obligation to philanthropy is subordinated to privatized care unless public care is legislated as the national framework of the healing arts and sciences. But as long as medical education is set in the market ethos, even socialized medical care remains subject to greed among its practitioners, as well as exploitation by pharmaceutical and technological suppliers.

What is needed to align the healing covenant and its medical code is a concept of the physician's *indebtedness* to the society that transmits the institution of medicine from age to age, a debt far greater than the unreturnable social investment from which an individual physician – or any other professional agent – benefits. It is a debt that is expressed only in honouring the covenant between doctors and their teachers, among whom must be counted their patients from whose suffering the physician's trade is also learned and with whom the covenant of care is most lively. Contract medicine erodes this covenant, aggravating the doctor-patient relationship with defensive malpractice litigation (increasingly an issue for other professions), which in turn breeds further contractualism beyond what is required by sound practice.

Civic Vigilance and Urbanity

The health of a society is not due to its medical institutions. Rather, medicine itself is indebted to the civic health of the society in which it is practised. A covenant theory of institutions therefore requires of us a practice of civic witness extended to the mutual care of persons and things in their wholeness and integrity. Civic witness is exercised in seeing things round, in celebrating time and place, nativity and burial, and the endurance of their corporeal bonds. The saving of the particular events and frail connections of the human family and its extended community is work that rests upon a variety of faiths. It may be practised both by the social planner and by the social worker. The problem is how to see the look in the eye and how to listen to what we hear in the sounding of human care. This is achieved in our openness to the belonging together of our own senses and our civic life that offers us the possibility of munificence. Our humanity is properly exercised in our orientation to the embodied community that is our destiny or allotment. Care, then, is the domicile of our being together (Heidegger 1960). This indwelling institutes a civic connection between the eye, the ear, the heart, and the mind of the citizen within the greater body-politic that may heal their wounds in the strength of time. Thus, we include in our capacity for witness a capacity for transgression. But in our capacity for transgression we include our prayer for forgiveness. Thus civic witness does not demand liberal compliance any more than it reserves redemption for successful conformity. By the same token, anyone can violate the civic order – not only youth, not only males – just as anyone can defend it – not only the politically correct.

The civic witness we have in mind is particularly relevant to the condition of our cities, which are so easily undermined by the corporate monuments that dominate their streets, erasing the small events that generate civic life. The sensory deprivation, squalor, and violence that are experienced in the declining cities of market society must also be understood in terms of the decline of the corporeal covenant that was once operative on the street level. For, as Jane Jacobs (1961) has shown so well, the city is a form of life, a daily composition of the human senses whose architecture is the product of both civic and professional eye-work. The aesthetics of the city – so depleted in suburbia and the shopping mall – are the result of the interplay between the situated vision of citizens involved in their daily pursuits and the professional vision of urban designers. The relation between these two aesthetics can only be neglected at the cost of the political life of the city. The difference in the virtues of these two modes of eye-work is vital to the perception of civic order and beauty, as well as to the tension and insecurity produced by disorder and ugliness in the cityscape.

Any attempt to institute control of streets, parks, and neighbourhoods is unlikely to confirm the everyday visual order of neighbourhood life. Here the absence of civic witness is to be found in the proliferation of signs and notices with which we police the missing community. Moreover, to the extent that official surveillance is at all successful, it rests upon the everyday eye-work of responsible citizens and neighbours. It is our routine comings and goings, shoppings, loiterings, and conversations that provide the 'eye-catchers' for trouble, the unusual, accidents, losses, and injury. On every occasion that something out of the ordinary catches a neighbour's eye, as a matter she or he treats with responsible concern, there occurs a reinforcement of civic order and of everyone's competence with the collective expectation of its preservation.

Public propriety involves us not simply in the pursuit of our own business; it engages us in a watchful concern for others who in turn keep an eye on our own course. The vitality of our city streets contributes to the exercise of civic witness and is thereby an essential factor in the good governance of urban life. The agency of this order is as subtle as a fleeting glance and as tenacious as the looks of neighbours, elders, and policemen. What sustains this civic scene is everyone's openness and shared responsibility for the contingencies of street conduct. Unless participation in greeting, directing, watching, and helping others on the street is assumed, along with one's own right of way, the path is soon fraught with danger. Here, then, we have a further exercise in the covenant of care that is vital to our children. For the look and feel of our city streets is an icon of our social and political life. It is also a source of personal harmony and aesthetic satisfaction to children as well as adults. Ugliness and violence in the streets threatens us not only in a bodily way; it is an injury to our civic pride. For the city is in ruin when it looks ugly and feels dangerous. Yet the city cannot be saved from ruin merely by design. The architect's vision should not be more privileged that the citizen's vision, schooled by what we see around us everyday. We behold the city in the course of our daily round and even the view from its highest rooftop is only one more view offered by the city's embrace. But those who love the city are not its passive spectators or its busy tourists. Those who love the city are those who take care of its streets with an eye for what goes on and for who goes there.

When citizens fear to look one another in the eye or when they look upon their neighbours with indifference, the city is indeed in ruin. Today, everyone may fear for themself in our cities and towns. The particular horrors of a kidnapping, a child murder, the rape and murder of our women, or the robbery and beating of our elder citizens are aggravated when our police are either themselves the victims or else the aggressors in the conduct of keeping the peace. Whenever anyone of us, regardless of age, sex, or race is at risk we are all at risk. This is because the young and the old, males and females, the married and unmarried, the rich and poor are not two or more kinds of beings, but truly elements of our common corporeal condition that binds us to common joys and common sufferings that cry out for a common peace and common justice. This, then, is the thread of child, family, community, and state governance that must be woven tightly if we are to clothe ourselves in civility and care.

FIVE

Three Reciprocity Lessons

The civic covenant we have elaborated so far derives from basic moral principles that we will set out in Three Lessons of Reciprocity (the R-Lessons). These lessons constitute a civil reminder that any form of sustainable society is grounded in a vast lore/law that requires us to extend ourselves in a community of civic obligation towards others whose recognition simultaneously affords us our own moral worth.

A Covenant Critique of Rawls on Future Justice

Although John Rawls (1971) does consider the problem of intergenerational reciprocity in his classical treatise on contractarian justice, his assumptions are peculiar when viewed from the standpoint of the covenant concept of embodied obligations:

1 Rawls starts from 'nobodies,' that is, entities in an 'original position' of 'ignorance' with regard to any self-characteristic such as age, income, or family relation, and of 'disinterest' with regard to the general good and their own future.

2 Since all such bodies are the 'same' body, they unanimously agree to a social contract (in what sense can one body be considered 'social'?) whose basic principles are:

    a. Each person is to have an equal right to the most
extensive basic liberty compatible with a similar liberty for others (again, what sense can be given to
'others' by 'one' body?).

    b. Social and economic inequalities are to be arranged so
that they are both (i) to the greatest benefit of the least
advantaged and (ii) attached to offices and positions
open to all under conditions of fair equality of opportunity.

3 All social values are to be distributed equally unless it is
to everyone's advantage that there be inequality with
respect to some values. (How, then, can equality be considered an overriding value, since it is quite possible that
it may be a disvalue – the same being true of inequality;
so must not social justice be a higher value than the pres-
ence/absence of equality/inequality?)

Now the last assumption (the difference principle) entirely
rules Rawls's concept of future justice, since it requires an
overriding choice of values that will improve the welfare of
the 'worst-off' citizens in future generations. But it is difficult
to find any imaginative basis for such comparison, because
Rawls's citizen is the 'same' body at time T_1 as at time T_2.
'S/he' has an equal probability of being any citizen, but has no
specific knowledge either of them or of 'hirself' under a variety of moral and political situations. But then, of course, 'she'
cannot interpret '*hir*' possible surroundings because 's/he' has
no sentiments or embodied relations that are ground for understanding the possible effects of 'hir' choices. Rawls's citizen
is an homogenized entity and 'hir' fate, supposing 's/he' could
consider it, would seem to be the principal failure of Rawl's
scheme for saving liberal contract theory.

Worse still, Rawlsian society is in effect a static society,
since the difference principle does not allow present savings
that might improve future generations. To avoid this state of
affairs, Rawls is obliged to *familize* his citizens by making

their attitude towards future generations analogous to their attitude towards their own children. But then future generations cannot be modelled after the parent's interest in the child without some further assumption about the child's interest in the parent. In short, Rawls once again lacks any embodied ground for a calculus regarding future generations. Even when we vary the model to one in which we imagine ourselves doing what we think the next generation would have done for us (Mueller 1974), we still assume a single-body 'society.'

A future generation never stands as a single body in relation to a present body, as required by contractarian principles, since each generation is composed of an extraordinary variety of bodies whose circumstances overlap in the seamless web of moral and political life. In other words, the commitments and obligations of everyday political life already precede any liberal scenario of contract and consensus. A considerable fiction is required to reduce the embodied overlap of *intra*generational and *inter*generational institutions to the terms of a two-party contract. Indeed, one can only suppose that the extraordinary intellectual effort that goes into the contractarian fiction is required by its need to underwrite its fundamental libertarianism, that is, its belief that the burden of society could only have been self-imposed under circumstances that in effect permit us to write off its costs due to the expansiveness of an egalitarian economy that is careful not to hamper liberty with equality – not now and not in the future (Barry 1973; Daniels 1975; Martin, 1985). The alternative is to conceive of a radical institutional change whereby the allocation of welfare between generations is made by a body removed from current values and control (Mueller et al. 1974). Such a device, however, owes more to economistic policy thinking than to the nature of the political process and the current pluralism that now shapes demands for social justice and ecological care.

We are therefore drawn further into the exercise of re-addressing the grounds of civic reciprocity and the nature of the founding covenant that underwrites the welfare ethic in modern times. The R-Lessons are no one's property because they are everyone's cultural legacy contained in myth, religion, folk tales, and theatre, as well as in primal scenes of everyday moral accountability acted out by each one of us in the great school of life and work, in our homes and our community, in childhood, in old age, in health and in sickness, towards ourselves and towards others who are like ourselves in respect of their adherence to this great covenant.

Lesson One is that reciprocity does not have to be taught formally but is absorbed through civic institutions that both endow and indebt each one of us.

Lesson Two is that because the market systematically produces moral strangers, the principles and practices of reciprocity must be embedded in civic institutions that sustain common care without exclusion.

Lesson Three is that civic institutions must be grounded in both intragenerational and intergenerational reciprocity towards the past and towards the future of which we are trustees.

So far from being narrowly familistic, the reciprocity lessons require of us an ethic of hospitality – of the stranger's, the ancestor's, and the newborn's welcome home. The stranger is one whose difference we respect rather than fear. The ancestor and the unborn are to be welcomed into our lives rather than driven out. To be practised effectively, the reciprocity lessons demand not only moral imagination but also political solidarity expressed in the delegation of our will not to exclude anyone from agency within our civic institutions – present, past, and future. We know of no political institution other than the welfare state that can bring to bear upon citizens in need the intent of our solidarity with one another. This work is under way. No political party has a monopoly on the vision required to produce a viable second-generation welfare state in Canada. But without such a vision there can be no hope for a sustainable society whose goal must be an end to the indifferent loss of family and employment that destroys the future of our children and youth.

It is a curiosity of market ethics that its logic of selfishness does not discount its potential rewards with the sacrifices involved, for example, in weakening public security and in suffering random violations of person and property. Surely, it is odd to refuse the practice of altruism on the ground that public generosity involves the sacrifice of uniquely selfish motives, whereas it is the practice of selfishness that sacrifices personal and public freedom to the insecurity and violence inherent in the degradation of civic institutions:

> The question, then, is how different moral codes come to recognize and value the many small gifts of everyday life that reinforce the social order. The problem with reliance on the market as a moral code is that it fails to give moral credit to those whose sacrifices enable others to consider themselves freely choosing agents. By concentrating on the good news that we can improve our position, rather than the not-so-good, but socially necessary, news that we might consider the welfare of others as our direct concern, the market leaves us with no way to appreciate disinterest. (Wolfe 1989: 102)

The civic work of showing how society is a fabric of intragenerational and intergenerational fates cannot be left to the market-place. This is not because the market will neglect the public sphere, but precisely because it is concerned only with its manipulation on behalf of possessive consumerism and political docility. We cannot count upon the state to underwrite our civic culture unless we also resist our current temptation to divest the state's civic-welfare functions in the name of global competition, which serves to abet duty-free corporations. Nor should we attempt to dismantle the welfare state that we have so freely abused in order to bring our house in order through a single-generation correction of the national deficit. Here, as elsewhere, the language of sacrifice is used to mobilize at home what is in effect industrial genocide inflicted on the young to make way for a new global combination of wealth and poverty. It is this shift that in our opinion constitutes the much-heralded shift from modernity to postmodernity. Globalism, however, does not release the energy of an old-order modernity limited by its reluctance to entirely subordinate the polity to the economy – as is claimed in the rhetoric of free trade and economic community. What is released by civic-free globalism is the moral spring that held national wealth and poverty in some balance; what is released is the moral balance between the young and the elderly, between the healthy and the sick; and what snaps is the civic tension that holds together our materialism and our idealism. What we lose in the new combination of duty-free globalism and postmodern amoralism is any memory – let alone imagination – of that civic commons apart from which society falls into a series of fortresses surrounded by hovels. Lit only by the light of television, rather than by an alternative theatre of hope and justice that has carried human history through the darkest hours, our homes become caves (O'Neill 1992).

Lesson One: The Norm of Reciprocity

Every society ritualizes the exchange relationships through which it sustains its civility:

> There are certain duties that people owe one another, not as human beings, or as fellow members of a group, or even as occupants of social statuses within the group but rather, because of their prior actions. We owe others certain things because of what they have previously done for us, because of

the history of previous interaction we have had with them. It is this kind of obligation which is entailed by the generalized norm of reciprocity. (Gouldner 1960: 170–1)

In everyday life we are all participants and witnesses to rituals of reciprocity that celebrate exchanges between society, nature, and God, invoking a covenant between them as the model of all other civic reciprocities between individuals, neighbours, families, communities, and the state. By the same token, violations, neglect, and abandonment of the rituals of reciprocity are abhorred. Every society institutionalizes what we may call the R-Lessons in its great texts – in its works of ethics, religion, law, literature, theatre, and opera, as well as in folklore, fairy tales, cartoons, and movies. Every generation learns what we may call *R-Lesson One* at home, at school, at play, at work, in love. Anyone who has not heard of R-lesson One, or who has but does not believe it and refuses to practise it, risks not being one of us. That is the lesson of reciprocity. It ought to provide the basic staple of our schools and universities.

However the first lesson of reciprocity is defined in the conduct of society, economy, and polity, it is taken to be 'known' by all:

Ignorance of the law/lore of reciprocity is not to be invoked by anyone with a claim to moral membership.

By the same lore, violations of reciprocity are assumed to be recognizable and reparable, either in kind or by communication, and so far as possible without litigation or force (Becker 1986). R-Lesson One must not be considered familistic or limited to traditional notions of upbringing that no longer rule market society (Godbout 1992). Nor should we imagine that the claims of reciprocity can be monetized so that it is possible to buy out from one's social debts to the family and to the community at large. Yet many people are tempted to think that through the reluctant payment of taxes and professional fees they may delimit their commitments to the larger civic arena that enables their private lives. They imagine that individuals might live among one another as civil 'strangers,' with only so much mutual care and recognition of one another as is filtered through the institutions – school, police, medicine, charity, social work, and welfare – that 'we' subscribe to through taxation in one form or another.

Lesson Two: No Moral Strangers

Nothing so violates the civic covenant as the market production of moral strangers – the vulnerable, the sick, the unemployed, and the criminal. Moreover, nothing so depletes the civic treasury as the drain upon it to police, confine, and conscript young men (and now young women) on behalf of the property system that excludes them. Nothing else so distorts our well-being as the system of health and justice that is afforded in a market society. Therefore, we must formulate a second reciprocity lesson as follows:

The more distant universal exchange systems become, the more principles and practices of reciprocity must be embedded in civic institutions that sustain common care.

What is involved here is a shift in the civic structure of embodied care necessitated by the other shifts in family demography, neighbourhoods, and medicalized care discussed in previous chapters.

'We are responsible *for* each other,' 'but we are not responsible *to* each other,' says Ignatieff (1984: 10; my emphasis). In a sense, because of the complexity of modern exchange, we seek to narrow our immediate touch in favour of extending our collective embrace of one another's needs in infancy, old age, sickness, disability, distress, and unemployment. We are aware that our moral person is not capable of meeting our collective commitments unless we delegate ourselves in the person of volunteers, social workers, and health-care professionals whose immediate touch with those in need extends our own moral reach: 'It is this solidarity among strangers, this transformation through the division of labour of needs into rights and rights into care that gives us whatever fragile basis we have for saying that we live in a moral community' (ibid.).

But the civic community itself is the principal need we recognize on behalf of one another, and it is from this civic need that the language of other needs for food, shelter, health, education, and employment is to be derived. We may say, further, that the civic community is an embodied community whose potential satisfaction in any particular case is diminished wherever another goes in need:

Individuals are not solitary masters of pre-given preferences; what others need and what they lack are constitutive of their own needs. It is as common for us to need things on behalf of others, to need good schools for the sake of our children, safe streets for the sake of our neighbours, decent old people's homes for the strangers at our door, as it is for us to need them for ourselves. The deepest motivational springs of political involvement are to be located in this human capacity to feel needs for others. (Ibid.: 17)

It is important, as we have argued throughout, not to allow the colonization of the civic community by the secondary institutions of care and welfare that it generates, since in its particular practices the welfare system may well violate the solidarity it is intended to service (Jordan 1987). Moral solidarity is inherent in both our primary and secondary institutions of care; it charges both institutions with the cultivation of our civic covenant and the care of others in need.

We cannot separate the first two lessons of reciprocity. It is not possible to have a responsive civic community that many now call for without it being funded by the civic covenant that derives from positive community/state reciprocity. Each must rekindle the other. These assertions do not arise from a persistent nostalgia, nor from an obstinate traditionalism. They are not the battle-cry of fundamentalism. They arise because there is already a 'crisis' on the side of the state and professional welfare systems. This crisis of 'overload' – generated by fiscal restraints and withdrawals of collective reciprocity – exists even where the state therapeutic complex never came close to absorbing the kin/community care system. Although it had earlier sought to delegitimize community care with the aim of eventual colonization, the welfare state would have experienced an even deeper fiscal crisis had the kin/community care system modernized itself to become completely monetized and professionalized. Now, however, any move to offload state care onto kin/community care practices presupposes that they have in fact withstood previous attempts to delegitimize and destroy our civic legacy in them.

Lesson Three: The Norm of Reciprocity within and between Generations

Having argued for the inseparability of the first two lessons of reciprocity, we must now argue for a third lesson:

Civic sustainability must be grounded in both intra-generational and inter-generational reciprocity.

We cannot, of course, ground the claims of intergenerational justice in families without a correspondingly intergenerational concept of family foundation and commons. That is the point of our earlier recovery of the concept of the covenant family in chapter 3. Without this exercise, family life may be considered merely another basis for shortsighted self-interest locked in a zero-sum game against other families, or as an institution of local benevolence enjoyed without regard for the universal citizen who is our modern other – let alone any concern for unborn generations beyond blood lines. Another benefit of the covenant model of the intergenerational family that we introduced earlier is that it takes the weight off futuristic scenarios regarding the claims of 'possible' or 'unborn' people inasmuch as in the intergenerational model every present family, was once a future family so that from the continuity thereby achieved we have less reason than do procreative contractarians to think of future beings as 'non-selves,' or 'aliens' whose utility-functions might well be beyond our ken. In short, the covenant family grounds its civic imagination in its memory, whereas the sexual-contract family can only contemplate fresh starts without any previous understandings since it is constituted by its sovereign will to abandon past memories and future obligations. The covenant family, by contrast, can contemplate without contradiction the claims upon its munificence of both past and future generations.

It is not necessary to reduce intergenerational reciprocity to a two-person contract in order to rationalize its benefits, as do liberal utilitarians like Rawls (1971). The logic of two-person pacts requires an exemption from any such encumbrances as are recognized in our concern for past and future generations as parties to our own present (Laslett and Fishkin 1992). The covenant family, we argue, must therefore act towards *itself*, as well as towards past and future families, in terms of a moral trust imposed upon it by the past and by posterity. It is, however, no part of our trusteeship to exhaust or to divide up the legacy into which we have been born, for it far exceeds any concept of property and the legal discourse we have constructed upon it. Moreover, since we should have enjoyed nothing from the past had it abrogated to itself the depletion of its 'own' cultural legacy, we ought to extend such forbearance to ourselves just as we ought to secure the lives of future children in response to our own past gift of life and protection against our dependency and vulnerability. For the same reason, a covenant society rejects the technological power available to the present generation that makes it possible to contemplate – and hence necessary to forbear – the destruction of the two worlds of man and nature (O'Neill 1992). Since all future life – with the possible exception of the cockroach's – is vulnerable, we ought to begin to cultivate a duty towards our own offspring as well as towards the fruits and animals of nature.

The three reciprocity lessons are grounded in the embodied imagination of the collectivity whose members are born, age, marry, and die together, each in their turn and without exception. In this sense, civic society is founded upon a 'covenant of covenants' irreducible to any rational-legal contract we may make to facilitate our affairs. Properly speaking, marriage, birth, and death are *not* contracts, although they may be attended by devices requiring contracts, such as contraception, abortion, divorce, and euthanasia. Rather, Life, Love, and Death are moments in a Covenant through which we are entered into civic institutions that entirely surpass each one of us, even though they provide for our unique value.

Now it is a paradox of the three R-Lessons that if they are taught well enough, civic reciprocity will appear voluntary. But if these lessons are only voluntary their results may not be 'good enough.' Therefore, it will be necessary – for the sake of any future – to devise welfare strategies that will serve to underwrite our *covenantal imagination*. For unless what everyone wants is so funded that no one is excluded or driven into an underclass, or into dependency and self-exempting disability, the goodness of civil society is made brittle. Before long there are tears in the social fabric and there are found in the streets unfortunate and unsightly persons upon whom we turn that blind eye which diminishes our own moral vision.

SIX

Life Chances within a Civic Commons

The covenant concept of life chances and opportunities represents a more generous affirmation of what is owed to children and youth than either the scarcity-bound concept of basic needs or the market-driven concept of individual autonomy achieved in a society that continuously reproduces failure and dependency. The limitation of the opposition between autonomy and dependency is that each condition is defined with respect to the welfare state but without reference to their common origin in the successes and failures of the market. The loss of civic status becomes a risk run by individuals whose luck in the market determines the moral status of their families and children. By contrast, in the covenant concept of opportunity, civic institutions are regarded as a commons that fosters individual talent without any initiating rituals of failure and exclusion. The provision of culture is grounded in past and future obligations that are exercised in the affirmation of the continuity of good-enough institutions of health, education, and work along with the civil institutions that redeem our misfortunes inasmuch as we must also care for, cure, and police ourselves.

Civic-free global capitalism threatens to devour the world's children. It demands that each nation sacrifice their schooling and their employment to its greedy machines that apprentice them to information without knowledge and consumption without joy. It separates the lives of children into the two worlds of poverty and affluence; it breaks the bond between children and society and between their families. Thus, the market already conscripts our high-school and university students to consumerism, which they underwrite through part-time work whose demands render them part-time students at best. The questionable results of such a system of de-schooling now produce calls for the nationalization of schooling in response to global competition. The civic degradation of our schools and universities is another effect of the market's separation from the polity. Yet these events are not the effects of any political conspiracy, nor of the irresistible force of the market – and certainly not the inevitable outcome of overburdening welfarism. Each nation must accept responsibility for its own harshness towards children and youth and for its failure to strengthen the civic commons that has for half a century softened the discomforts of class-based poverty and prejudice. If ever we lose sight of the civic commons that is at risk in the debate over the welfare state, we truly risk returning to that state of nature where life is short, nasty, and brutish – as it still is, despite the claims of the market to have delivered us once for all into security and well-being.

Children for Sale

We must resist the moods of the market that drive the cycle of excess and depletion in our lives. We must defend ourselves against the breakdown of health and knowledge, of peace and security due to the excesses of medicine, schooling, and policing that result in fiscal crises which, paradoxically, are regarded as signs of the need to return to market accountability. Swings in rates of employment, wages, mortgages, credit, and government transfer payments constantly erode the thin line between civility and barbarism for large sectors of the population. It is this border that is crossed when we read that in Canada *15 to 20 per cent* of children live in poverty, or that *over a million* people are unemployed, among whom *nearly 20 per cent* are youths.

On the international level, the vocabulary of 'basic human needs' is particularly fraught with the market fantasy of material survival in a world without any covenant to alter the endless destruction of children. Consider the following item (*Globe and Mail*, 30 October 1993):

LIFE IS CHEAP

In 1955, Canadian children first began collecting money for the United Nations Children's Fund on Halloween night. A generation later, as they prepare to send their own children out the door with an orange-and-black Unicef box, many must be wondering what it has accomplished. Children around the world still die of malnutrition and disease in huge numbers – about 35,000 a day, according to Unicef. A sense of hopelessness attends the campaign to save these children, a feeling that (as a recent Unicef report put it) 'the effort to end the worst evils of absolute poverty has been tried and failed.' Wrong on both counts, argues the report, The Progress of Nations: it has not been tried; and it has not failed.

Despite the UN's efforts, just 10 per cent of international development aid goes to basic health needs: nutrition, primary health care, water and sanitation, primary education and family planning. That works out to $4-billion a year – less than half what the aid-giving countries spend each year on sports shoes.

Yet even that small sum has accomplished miracles. In little more than one generation, says Unicef, 'child death rates have been more than halved; malnutrition rates have been reduced by about 30 per cent; life expectancy has increased by about a third; the proportion of children enrolled in primary school has risen from less than half to more than three quarters; and

Save the children

It is no longer possible to say that meeting basic human needs is too vast or expensive a task. With present knowledge, it could be done within a decade and at a cost of an extra $25-billion per year. Some comparisons:

Cigarettes in Europe (per year) — 50
Business entertaining in Japan (per year) — 35
Beer in the USA (per year) — 31
Russian 1992 G7 aid package — 27
Proposed new Hong Kong airport — 23
Meeting basic needs (per year) — 25

billions of $US
Source: UNICEF

the percentage of families with access to safe water has risen from less than 10 per cent to more than 60 per cent.'

If we have learned anything in this effort, it is that saving children is remarkably cheap. A mere 14 cents will provide a package of oral rehydration salts to a child suffering from dehydration due to diarrhea. One dollar will immunize 30 toddlers against diphtheria, whooping cough and tetanus.

Low-cost strategies such as these already save more than four million children a year. Unicef estimates that within a decade, it should be possible to reduce child deaths by a further four million a year, to halve child malnutrition, to bring clean water and sanitation to all communities, to provide basic education for all children and to control the major childhood diseases. The cost of this giant leap in human progress: about $25-billion a year (see chart).

Against that sum, the pennies, dimes and quarters collected by trick-or-treaters do not seem like much. But the $4-million Unicef hopes to raise on Halloween is enough to immunize 300,000 children. Tomorrow night, remember those orange-and-black boxes.

The report of 35,000 daily deaths from disease and malnutrition among children represents the most extraordinary genocidal and intergenerational sacrifice we know. Yet it is constructed upon a crude economistic trope regarding the cheapness of life, despite the fact that we entirely lack the sentiment, or charity, or political will to buy off infant mortality even for a few cents a day (Benthall 1993). Moreover, our own children will have had several dollars' worth of candy, and even more dollars spent on costumes to enjoy Halloween night – yet most of them will be without the UNICEF boxes into which the hopes of another 35,000 dying children might have gone. But what is morally repulsive in all this is the notion that any part of humanity might place a price upon the lives of any other part, and even set it low enough to pay itself back with the claim that we thereby make 'a giant leap in human progress.' Nothing is said of the shame in such matters; no blame is attached to the barbarity of the world's nations who continue to destroy their own children; nothing is said about a world in which UNICEF never goes out of business.

Youth versus Elders

In the last fifty years the welfare state has functioned to spread income over the life cycle of citizens who might not have had the foresight to do this for themselves, and it has set up the expectation that every generation would at a later age benefit from the contributions it made when younger to its contemporary elders (Hills et al. 1993). However, there is evidence (Johnson et al. 1989; Thomson, 1991) that this exercise in intergenerational reciprocity has been violated. In New Zealand and elsewhere, including Canada, government policies on full employment, tax relief, mortgages, health, and education have benefited the generations between 1930 and 1960. Thereafter, governments have gradually reduced or withdrawn elements of the welfare system, with the result that it is now the principal source of the well-being of the contemporary elderly while extending far fewer benefits to contemporary youth (McKie, 1993). In short, there may be a breach of intergenerational reciprocity that results from the welfare system being overused and undersubscribed by previous generations at the cost of today's youth and tomorrow's elders.

> The glorification of self-interest, and denigration of collective activity, represent to many a stunning and bewildering reversal of the ideology of a few decades ago, when the new welfare state was erected to control these very evils. It is a reversal, but it does not mean that the welfare state has been 'hijacked' or has lost its way; it has simply evolved as it would and must. A system of pooling, intended to relieve personal anxiety and to turn thoughts to the community good instead works over time to the opposite end. Moreover, as it becomes clear that the common is being depleted, and that future benefits from it must shrink, then a switch toward an individualistic ideology becomes attractive. That means that we can each justify the personal gain already made at the expense of the pool, and yet cut future obligations to contribute. (Thomson 1991: 206).

This is the crux of the contemporary welfare crisis to which some respond with recommendations for more cuts that will reduce even further the life chances of those whose place is vulnerable inside and outside of the market. The combined effect of increased unemployment and reduced earnings among youth is a major source of their political distrust and cultural alienation from adult society. Of course, it would be a serious error to interpret this intergenerational split apart from the dual economy of the rich and poor that the globalization of the market forces upon national economies. Nor should we over-look how young people are sold on amusements and escapes that convey hard-line ideologies of self-assertion, sexual free-dom, and consumption in a world where their prospects are more and more bleak. The other side of this situation is youth violence, murder, and suicide, which call forth police and im-prisonment as the response of a society that will amuse youth but is not amused by youth. Even where young adults are busy with two jobs, a mortgage, a car on credit, and children need-ing child care, it may be argued that they must be counted among the 'new poor.' Their collective futures are as imper-illed as those of unemployed youth, since they all face a future in which the foundations of our civic institutions will be erod-ed, with even greater burdens placed upon their market achievements:

> The 'future prospects' portion of the packages of rewards for work are quite unalike for different generations. Those who were young workers in the 1950s and 1960s, for example, lived in a society which was investing heavily in the future, was relatively free of debt and was promising that the powers of the state would be used to advance their interests. Their successors, already collecting substantially lower real incomes at the same stage in life, face much more severely constrained 'future pros-pects'. The income they can expect for the rest of their lives must be limited by the under-investment and debt accumulation of the last 20 or so years. Moreover, they face governments which, through actions and now words, are telling them repeat-edly that they are not intent upon protecting, let alone advanc-ing, their interests. (Thomson 1991: 119–20).

It is the combined effect of structural changes in the global economy and the depletion of the welfare state that must be understood as the context for the apparent contradiction of greedy young consumers and apathetic young citizens. The difference between the conformism and the alienation of young people derives from their relative place in the market and the schools that serve to feed them into it. By the same token, the overburdening and the disenfranchisement of youth may be expected to recruit them to neoconservatism insofar as it locates their troubles in the burden of taxes and the threat of immigrants, or any other group vulnerable to the release of aggression. Unfortunately, the public acts of crime and violence that will attract attention to youth will do more to exclude them from citizenship than to raise public intelligence on the causes of the destruction of their future. Meantime the wider society is diverted by the struggle to deal with employment, delaying parenting, combining work and parenting, and single parenting with-or-without work. Those with jobs have also to face the prospect of more frequent job loss, job-sharing, and a shorter working life imposed through earlier retirement. Thus, there is a considerable 'downsizing' or depletion of the realm of civic life afforded in the new economy, which will be even less generous if we remove the welfare state. Should this occur, the bond between classes and generations will have been broken and late capitalism will unleash all the incivility of what we have called the duty-free society.

The relevance of the distinction we have drawn between liberal civil society and the covenant concept of civic society, is clear once we bring it to bear upon the practice of care for others whose market position renders them vulnerable to neglect. Because liberalism privatizes civic society it reduces its care practices to those of self-provision, insurance, and tax remittances that go to provide for the needs of strangers whose civic exclusion is confirmed by the stigma of welfare. This unhappy market concept of the civic stranger is even less fortunate when extended to the care of future generations, towards whom our moral obligations can hardly be pictured in terms of our present care of either the young or the elderly.

We increasingly raise children in poverty and are tempted to pit their claims against the claims of the elderly in an intergenerational war. All the trends that weaken family and community resources aggravate the niggardliness of liberal civility and remove us ever further from the provision of the resources that sustain an intragenerational and intergenerational civic covenant. What the market does is to reduce the temporal horizons of the family to instant gratifications eked out by credit payments. Consumerism pits the generations against one another. The all-knowing media child is the corporate terminal in families and schools without authority (O'Neill 1991). Such children are accustomed to all the scarcities that derive from the outstripping of family income by family outgo, including their own part-time incomes. The result is that their own childhood is shortened, while its quality is thinned. Later, their youth and adulthood is harassed by scarcities that make them mean towards their own children and elders. To accommodate to these amoral arrangements, elders disavow their claims upon family care while their grandchildren are fed with counterpart discourses of empowerment and rights. Thus, civic society is hollowed out with the uncivil language of the self's obligations towards itself and the market's identification of autism with altruism. Because these trends prevail by separating individuals from their past as well as their future, individuals are all the more bound to an ignorant present without either presence or perspective. These are the parameters of the thin self and its substitute practices of family, school, and community that characterize liberal civility in the absence of any understanding of the civic covenant that sustains authentic relations between individuals and institutions.

The Covenant of Taxation

Our participation in the provision of the civic commons should not be held hostage by those who treat institutions as arenas of management practice, cash accountability, investment, and confiscation. The provision of the commons does not erode autonomy and rationality. Rather, it is the exercise of wild market freedoms that destroys that reasonable realm of civility where we affirm ourselves without necessary loss and injury to one another. Without such a realm, we cannot foster the well-being of all children and youth who have no ability to trade in the staples of their life and community. Nor can we protect them until we can prepare them for living in a world where the global market tests the foundations of every national community.

What we must do in Canada is to understand that the liberal ideology has relocated itself in the global market and then we must reaffirm our own covenant ideology. We must refurnish the civic commons in our own response as a global people whose welfare is larger than its market assessment and whose accommodation of diversity among families, communities, religions, and schools is rooted in our historical and political will to survivance. In this covenant we are collected but not collectivized. The promise of Canada is personal not private; we answer it through one another because each of us has enjoyed the trust of every other and none is either above or beneath the civic condition we hold in common. From the covenant standpoint it is clear that market power does not produce society because its economy is too feverish. Rather, it is society that produces power – but as a realm of peace, order, and good governance in which we can reflect upon our civic life with a view to action upon ourselves. Here we regard our civility as both foundation and effect of the polity from which our civic life flows without exhaustion, obliging us to enrich it rather than to deplete it.

Today, we witness a remarkable withdrawal from the civic

obligations that have been the foundation of the social commons. How is it that we now wonder whether we can afford schools, hospitals, theatres, parks, and public transportation? We do not hesitate to spend upon police and correction activities, whose agenda in fact derives from the deprivation of the domestic commons. Our current withdrawal from the obligations that continuously fund the civic commons threatens to return us to the very barbarous state of (man-made) nature from which the institution of the market is supposed to have delivered us. Civic institutions are not commodities to be produced or sold; they are not goods that some may possess while others are dispossessed of them. Institutions are richer than the needs they meet; they enrich us far beyond the autonomy they afford us. Institutions extend to each of us a promise of personal worth that far exceeds the exercise of individual ability; at the same time, they are far more charitable towards our inabilities and transgressions.

Civic institutions are not slot coin machines. We cannot play them; we should not gamble with them. Civic institutions are fostered through our contributions that are properly the expression of our rich right to give rather than of our mean duty to bear taxes, or to insist upon a shareholder's concept of the common good.

No one should be considered exempt from the reciprocities of everyday life. No one is too poor, too ignorant, too old or too young, too tired or too busy, too smart or too foolish to be excluded or to self-exempt from the countless ways in which each of us may be helpful, watchful, and concerned for one another. No one is too rich to self-exempt from making whatever contribution they can make to the social commons to which each of us is indebted for goods that cannot be reckoned, that cannot be saved unless they are given, and that cannot be enjoyed by us if not enjoyed by others.

The reciprocity lessons we advanced earlier are grounded neither in voluntarism nor in the fear of neglect. The absence of civic reciprocity cannot be provided for by any private scheme of insurance. Nor should the notion of inter-generational debt advanced in R-Lesson Three be framed as a 'tax' upon elders in favour of youth, or upon children in favour of elders – let alone as a donation from the privileged to the disadvantaged. R-Lesson Three instructs us in an 'institutional debt' or a covenant of gratitude that we acknowledge in ourselves and towards anyone else who in turn recognizes the civic legacy that endows all life with an absolute claim upon the collective expansion of life chances.

Therefore, in covenant theory we regard taxation as the civic exercise of reciprocity through which we recognize others who similarly extend themselves into and by means of social agencies acting on their behalf. From this point of view, citizens have a *right* to pay taxes (sustained, of course, by employment and health), just as they should have a moral right to care for one another's well-being and to take steps to reduce one another's suffering and inconvenience. The exercise of such civic rights and their confirmation is embodied in the social covenant and amplified in the extended agencies of the welfare state:

> The ways in which society organizes and structures its social institutions – and particularly its health and welfare systems – can encourage or discourage the altruistic in man; such systems can foster integration or alienation; they can allow the 'theme of the gift' (to recall Mauss's words) – of generosity towards strangers – to spread among and between social groups and generations. This ... is an aspect of freedom in the twentieth century which, compared with the emphasis on consumer choice in material acquisitiveness, is insufficiently recognized. (Titmuss 1970: 225–6)

Citizenship in the Civic State

It should be clear from recent debates that as long as we try to ground the welfare state in the liberal concept of civil society it will be perilously subject to swings in economic forces and political will that will at best afford it tolerance and at worst seek to sell it off (Offe 1988). The apologists of liberal welfare capitalism themselves recognize that it is questionable whether liberalism can summon the moral strength to solve its redistributive problem rather than stumble from crisis to crisis through its compulsion to maximize rather than socialize its goods production (Ellis and Kumar 1983). Even were one to accept the views of Hayek (1960) and Dworkin (1978) that liberal society must remain agnostic about the nature of the good life, it can be argued that certain basic needs would have to be met as a 'floor' to enable the pursuit of other goods. But this minimalist concept cannot be maintained for long without raising the redistributive problem in the affordance of the resources to meet the satisfaction of even basic needs.

In short, social justice requires the provision of civic staples available to every citizen whatever their place in the market. The true crisis of market liberalism lies in its inability to avoid creating the very social conditions that lead to a renewal, rather than to the disposal, of the welfare state (Hirsch 1977). Or, to put it another way, whenever market liberalism overrides the traditional limits of community, ethnicity, class, and religion, it acquires a barbarian face, abhorrent to any civilization. It is when liberal society adopts the extremes of selfishness that the state is dragged down into the pre-civil bog in which it is impossible to rescue ourselves from brute selfishness. It is otherwise clear that we have set limits to our selfishness and greed because we value trust and reciprocity for their own sake and not as secondary devices for protecting the greedy from the unwanted consequences of their greed. Thus, we do not have to defend the legitimacy of the welfare state as such – even though we seek to revise our conception of it. What we have to defend is the civic culture in which a welfare state is embedded.

It follows from the civic covenant that our current concept of citizenship must be strengthened. Citizenship is not exercised merely at the polls. Indeed, long before the electorate reaches the polls it has been alienated by the blatant manipulations of image politicians whose messages compete on the same level as other commercials for the dollar vote. Moreover, these messages currently seek to reduce the logic of social policy to the logic of economic policy, the latter shaped only by considerations of the citizen as an employee competing in a global market that is indifferent to the national polity. From this perspective, a broader concept of social citizenship is subject to a productivist critique on three fronts: namely, on the economic ground that it is too costly for economic growth; on the social ground that it demoralizes the working family by creating non-working dependents; and on the political ground that citizenship underwritten by welfare policy produces an underclass. Taken to the extreme, the productivist critique of social citizenship would result in an abandonment of the intergenerational bonds of citizenship on the ground that nothing is owed between those who are strong and those who are vulnerable in the market-place – a tendency that Canadian government policies have recently aggravated rather than eased.

Civic solidarity must be the basis of any adequate concept of citizenship and covenant. At the heart of civic solidarity is the state provision of unconditional staples that affirm community and kinship solidarity, which is still predominantly the work of families. Families make a huge civic contribution to the reduction of the harshness of economic inequality. Their contribution could not possibly be loaded onto state budgets any more than it can be converted to market agencies, where, of course, it would be priced beyond reach. In short, civic solidarity is based upon gift relationships that ultimately honour the principle of intergenerationality, cutting across age, gender, and class. Thus, no generation can sustain itself without recognizing its dependency upon a past and future social endowment which it in part inherits and to which it in part contributes. By the same token, civic society is depleted wherever the state is simply an agent of force on behalf of property rather than a moral agent on behalf of civic prosperity:

> The onus is on critics of the welfare state to suggest better ways of guaranteeing the satisfaction of human needs in face of the problem of moral hazard, rather than on the proponents of state welfare to justify their position further. The cost of adopting this position is that it brings home to the proponent of the welfare state the ambiguous excellence of state welfare. The welfare state is not just about the kindliness of meeting need. It is also about the exercise of state power to stop some people from doing what they would otherwise do, in the interests of equal rights. (Taylor-Gooby 1991: 213)

In more positive terms, we must imagine a dual economy of participation in both the material production and the civic production of a sustainable society served by each in accordance with the duties of membership and enjoyed by all in accordance with the rights of inclusion (Roche 1992). The civic needs of the commons call for the welfare state to re-endow the family economy. This cannot be achieved by ideological appeals to 'family values' that merely aggravate the division between relatively privileged families and vulnerable families. Such appeals are nothing but an apology for individualism in the name of the market family.

We cannot simply enjoy the high ground of the civic state unless we are willing to oppose ourselves on its behalf in the struggle against trans-state forces that continuously undermine civic sustainability and good governance. Two strategies are essential to civic sustainability: namely, to resist the economization of the political community, on the one hand, and to counter the depoliticization of citizenship, on the other hand. Fortunately, the docility of the ordinary citizen is never so complete as to close off these two strategies of civic struggle. But for citizenship to be effective the political covenant must be prior to all other conventions and contracts, because it funds everything that citizens owe to one another in the provision of civic security and well-being. We cannot subordinate our need for political community to other needs that are rendered or not by the market. This is because our very sense of what we need in the provision of civic life derives from our conviction that particular and general goods affirm the political covenant.

The priority of political goods over market goods does not depend upon the priority of the state over the individual; it derives from the fact that all goods – indeed, all bad things – are socially recognized. Moreover, the ability to share this perception, as well as to debate it within limits, is constitutive of civic identity and membership in the community. But the ability to share covenant values is not a test of individual talent; it is inherited by everyone with the historical and civic conditions that frame any political community. The recognition of the civic commons is fundamental to our conduct of the political debates through which we arrive at redistributions of the goods that affirm our well-being and the elimination or reduction of avoidable harms. Without recognition of the priority of the covenant over the contract concept of goods, everything for which there is a market may be considered a social good, whatever its effects upon the political community. Moreover, whatever the market does *not* produce and sell must also be considered to be without consequence for the community.

Whenever the political community subordinates itself to the market, it not only sacrifices those who are weak in the market to those who are strong, but it also sacrifices the public provision of civic diversity to the deprivation and depletion of the civic commons whose privatization and enclosure is imposed by the market.

The Canadian Commons

Given Canada's need to preserve its cultural legacy, through which we are disposed to embrace social obligations rather than individual rights, to modify contract and property law in favour of the preservation of the commons and its social programs, we must salvage the principal civic staples that were envisaged in the proposed 1992 amendments to the 1982 Constitution:

> The policy objectives set out in the provision on the social union should include, but not be limited to:
>
> – providing throughout Canada a health care system that is comprehensive, universal, portable, publicly administered and accessible;
> – providing adequate social services and benefits to ensure that all individuals resident in Canada have reasonable access to housing, food and other basic necessities;
> – providing high quality primary and secondary education to all individuals resident in Canada and ensuring reasonable access to post-secondary education;
> – protecting the rights of workers to organize and bargain collectively; and
> – protecting, preserving and sustaining the integrity of the environment for present and future generations. (Sullivan 1992)

The intent of the Charter provisions was to ensure for all Canadians a form of civic government dedicated to an inter-generational covenant between citizens of any circumstance and anywhere in Canada. As such, the legacy of Charlottetown was to give popular expression to the principles of universality, equalization, and regional equity that bind Canada to itself. By the same token, this national covenant is not simply a quixotic act of defiance against the global windmill. It is an act of national sovereignty that is in step with the United

Nations covenant on family and child provision. For this reason, Canada's dream of national survivance is not to be judged by global shrinkage but by the will of the world's nations to redeem the future of the world's families.

Individualism is an ideology that reflects the way capitalists regard property and the laws of property that assign to individuals their possessive concept of the use of social resources. Strictly speaking, the unit of capitalist society is the two-person contract through which individuals exercise their rights to mobilize their property. Wherever this contractual relationship is inviolate, it is because all the legal, social, and political institutions that it presupposes legitimate the system we recognize as a capitalist democracy. Contract, citizenship, bureaucracy, and the division between public and private capital are the basic elements of welfare-state capitalism. Contrary to the contemporary ideology of marketization, capitalism is unthinkable as solely private capital without the complement of public-capital expenditures that are both economically and politically essential to its legitimation. What is peculiar to the current concept of global capitalism is its attempt to invent for itself a return to a history that never existed, that is, to a time when the market was free of the state and civic encumbrances. This extraordinary concept of civic-free capitalism simultaneously engages in stripping itself of its civic obligations while demanding that the civic state also strip its social obligations towards future generations in line with responsible deficit management. These unprecedented demands are made in the name of the allegedly irresistible forces of global competition and free trade that demand market efficiency, achieved through the redesign of all our institutions – schools, hospitals, universities, arts, and sciences.

Globalization in effect constitutes a national industrial policy of deterritorialization and capital migration, abetted by anti-government ideology, designed to bring the national household in line with a family household that at its own level is devastated by structural unemployment, children without futures, and credit-serviced debt. In effect, the civic state is being torn apart by the demand that it withdraw its investments in civic capital, on the one hand, and that it sell off profitable public investments to private capital, on the other hand. These conflicting demands upon contemporary nation-states have already degraded the political, civic, and cultural environment that earlier capitalism understood to be essential to its legitimate operation – if only as a trade-off between its international operations and its national location (Wilson, forthcoming). In short, what is remarkable about global capitalism is its claim that it is capitalism that is essential to liberal democracy – even when it strips those democracies of their civic functions – whereas historically it is civic democracy that has been essential to the maintenance and growth of capitalism. In other words, we are not only downsizing business but also thinning the state in the name of good business – despite the progressive degradation and rebarbarization of both the domestic and international environments of global competition. Here neoconservatism courts neofascism by destroying the Keynesian social contract on employment, at the same time that it deepens consumer taxation – an agenda that risks domestic disaster in the name of the globalization of profit.

The conscription of even left democratic parties to the ideology that the state is the essential creator of national deficits through capital expenditures that are entirely market inefficient is the most extraordinary event in the historical relation between capitalism and democracy. What is all the more peculiar is that these notions are administered by the Bank of Canada, the IMF, and U.S. bond-rating companies whose pronouncements on capital flight are given accu-weather status (Sinclair 1993). This complex treats national economies in terms of a fictional household economy whose spendthrift ways are in fact unavoidable, because of low income, and too weak to spend us out of a recession. No one asks why business itself is still regarded as the norm for the operation of government at a time when business has less understanding of its own social presuppositions than ever and risks destroying the democratic basis without which it falls into a war zone.

The whole history of capitalism is the history of the establishment of the state of law and citizenship that enables capitalism's operations to be conducted and expanded in an environment that removes industry and agriculture from slavery. Thus, the state has been essential both to the provision of peace and order and to the inducement of economic development. Of course, capitalism has maintained a combative distinction between public and private capital, while benefiting from their complementarity and shifting the burden of taxation onto the public citizenry. It is therefore highly misleading to listen to current market ideologists upon the fruitlessness of 'public works' – as though the social infrastructure of capitalism were nothing but a make-work project for the flotsam and jetsam of global capitalism. It is indeed a curiosity of contemporary neoconservatism that it considers the disembedding of the economy from the polity a return to the original state of capitalism. In fact, capitalism could never have emerged without the shift in social institutions that we describe as the shift from feudalism to capitalism. But this shift did not institutionalize the private appropriation of capital without any corresponding civic duties required in recognition of the right to property. In other words, both the rights and duties of capitalists were understood to derive from society rather than nature – even in contract theory. Moreover, despite its vaunted independence, global capitalism is if anything now more dependent than ever upon the alignment of national states to secure its 'base' operations, which it hopes to maintain as enclaves or ghettos within national societies whose civic fabric it otherwise destroys.

In Canada our will to survivance and civic governance must be anchored in the sovereignty of a federal government whose public finances should frame and sustain the covenant through which Canadians have expressed their will to provide for one another. This will involve a general principle of fiscal responsibility, namely, the willingness of Canadians to accept marginally higher tax-rate levels, on the one hand, than those that prevail in the United States, but to levy corporate taxes that, on the other hand, take into account potential job destruction, given our border-relation. Yet these two aims are not in simple contradiction. This is because we know that if we cut back social provision rather than maintain it, we will deepen the current recession, in the short run, while in the long run we will have depleted the civic environment that underwrites industry. We believe that the uniquely Canadian option in the global market is the provision of a stable, high quality of life in a higher-tax society whose principal asset is attracting to itself global socio-economic benefits:

> In our 'continuing experiment with civilization', the next century will see a contest between societies that practise capitalism in a narrow laissez-faire context and societies that evolve capitalism in a broader social context. At present, the latter have a much better record of creating societies that have a broad base for individual and societal health and well-being. (Keating and Mustard 1993: 102)

We must therefore restate the covenant principles that should guide our current political debate:

1 The commons must not be subordinated to the market.
2 The polity must ensure the common provision of those civic goods whose enjoyment is sensible only when universal.
3 The polity must provide those universal goods that sustain our common obligation to meet the double claim upon us of social justice between contemporary generations and between the present and future generations.

The public life of the Canadian commons contains the

founding nations, new cultural and racial groups, as well as class and gender relations. It is composed of people of many creeds and with a variety of languages and customs that as Canadians they are learning to bring to bear upon the commons without dividing it into a set of warring tribalisms. The civic discourse of the commons must not, therefore, be reduced to any simple conflict between individual rights – or even group rights – and the state, any more than the state should homogenize its responses to the variety of claimants upon it. The commons is broader than either governments or individuals, and within it neither is privileged. It does not abandon private life to the market any more than it excludes government from interventions in social life because of any inherent rights either of states or of individuals. In this way, the commons is a reservoir of justice and hope for anyone and for all of us seeking remedy and well-being in Canada.

If Canada is to survive as a national community capable of responding to the political and economic forces gathering in the global market, we must reaffirm the civic foundations that are to sustain us without subordinating our political culture to the dominion of the market. We must consolidate the framework of values that has enabled us to place the civic covenant above the market contract and to derive from this common notion the following practices:

1 No one is outside of the commons.
2 The civic commons must not be sold off.
3 The provision of good-enough civic institutions does not burden us.
4 The impoverishment of our children and youth devastates us.
5 The provision of civic security is the ground of both our well-being and our freedom.
6 The covenant provision of sustainable civility must address two levels of civic reciprocity:
   a. *intra*generational justice

b. *inter*generational justice
that constitute our political and historical will to survivance.

We know already that apart from such a formula we will
continue to experience the vicious cycle of missing jobs, lost
wages and taxes, missing parental support, and lost youth. To
reverse this cycle, we must redistribute social demand rather
than contract it through reduction in family expenditures,
housing, schooling, and job training. If we fail to do so, we
will not be left with a leaner society hungry for global competition. We will be left with a meaner society – hostile alike to
capitalism and socialism. In such a society there will be no
place for the civic imagination – and no sound will be heard
from its children.

Political wisdom is not produced by the shock therapy of
market globalism. If we can rededicate the Canadian commons
to the well-being of the civic person who is already emerging
from our own political experience with global diversity, then
Canada will have contributed a model of survival and governance among the nations of the twenty-first century.

References

Agee, James, and Walker Evans. 1966. *Let Us Now Praise Famous Men*. New York: Ballantine Books

Arditti, Rita, et al. 1989. *Test-Tube Women: What Future for Motherhood?* London: Pandora Press

Banting, Keith G. 1987. *The Welfare State and Canadian Federalism*. Kingston and Montreal: McGill-Queen's University Press

– 1993. 'Economic Integration and Social Policy: Canada and the United States.' In Terrance M. Hunsley, ed., *Social Policy in the Global Economy*. Kingston: Queen's University School of Policy Studies

Barber, Benjamin R. 1984. *Strong Democracy: Participatory Politics for a New Age*. Berkeley: University of California Press

Barry, Brian. 1973 *A Liberal Theory of Justice*. Oxford: Clarendon Press

Beck, Ulrich. 1992. *Risk Society: Towards a New Modernity*. London: Sage Publications

Becker, Lawrence C. 1986. *Reciprocity*. London: Routledge and Kegan Paul

Bellah, Robert N., et al. 1992. *The Good Society*. New York: Vintage Books

Benhabib, Seyla. 1987. 'The Generalized Other and the Concrete Other: The Kohlberg-Gilligan Controversy and Moral Theory.' In Eva Feder Kittay and Diane T. Meyers, eds, *Women And Moral Theory*, 154–77. Totawa, NJ: Rowman and Littlefield

Benthall, Jonathan. 1993. *Disasters, Relief and the Media*. London: I.B. Tauris and Co.

Blustein, Jeffery. 1982. *Parents and Children: The Ethics of the Family*. New York: Oxford University Press

Bronfenbrenner, Urie. 1979. *The Ecology of Human Development: Experiments by Nature and Design.* Cambridge: Harvard University Press

Canadian Council on Social Development. 1988. *Perspective 2000.* Ottawa: Centre for International Statistics on Economic and Social Welfare

– 1993a. *Campaign 2000: Child Poverty in Canada Report Card 1993.* Centre for International Statistics on Economic and Social Welfare

– 1993b. *Countdown 93: Campaign 2000 Child Poverty Indicator Report.* Ottawa: Centre for International Statistics on Economic and Social Welfare

Cohen, Libby G. 1990. *Before Their Time: Fetuses and Infants at Risk.* Washington: American Association on Mental Retardation

Coleman, James S., Thomas Hoffer, and Sally Kilgore. 1982. *High School Achievement: Public, Private and Catholic High Schools Compared.* New York: Basic Books

Countdown 93: Campaign 2000 Child Poverty Indicator Report. 1993. Ottawa: Canadian Council on Social Development

Cragg, Wesley. 1986. 'Two Concepts of Community or Moral Theory and Canadian Culture.' *Dialogue* 25: 31–52

Dahrendorf, Ralf. 1959. *Class and Class Conflict in Industrial Society.* Stanford: Stanford University Press

– 1979. *Life Chances: Approaches to Social and Political Theory.* Chicago: University of Chicago Press

Daniels, Norman. 1975. *Reading Rawls.* New York: Basic Books

– 1988. *Am I My Parent's Keeper? An Essay on Justice Between the Young and the Old.* New York: Oxford University Press

De Coulanges, Fustel. 1901. *The Ancient City: A Study on the Religion, Laws, and Institutions of Greece and Rome.* Boston: Lothrop, Lee and Shepherd

Dizard, Jan E., and Howard Gadlin. 1992. *The Minimal Family.* Durham: Duke University Press

Drover, Glenn, and Patrick Kerans. 1993. *New Approaches to Welfare Theory.* Aldershot: Edward Elgar Publishing

Dryzek, John, and Robert E. Goodin. 1986. 'Risk-Sharing and Social Justice: The Motivational Foundations of the Post-War Welfare State.' *British Journal of Political Science* 16: 1–34

Durkheim, Emile. 1912/1954. *The Elementary Forms of the Religious Life.* London: Allen and Unwin

Dworkin, Ronald. 1978. 'Liberalism.' In Stuart N. Hampshire, ed., *Public and Private Morality,* 113–43. Cambridge: Cambridge University Press

– 1993. *Life's Dominion: An Argument about Abortion, Euthanasia, and Individual Freedom.* New York: Alfred Knopf

Ehrenreich, Barbara, and Deidre English. 1978. *For Her Own Good: 150 Years of the Expert's Advice to Women.* New York: Doubleday
Ellis, Adrian, and Krishan Kumar. 1983. *Dilemmas of Liberal Democracies: Studies in Fred Hirsch's* Social Limits to Growth. London: Tavistock Publications
Elshtain, Jean Bethke. 1982. *The Family in Political Thought.* Amherst: University of Massachusetts Press
– 1984. 'Reflections on Abortion, Values and the Family.' In Sidney Callahan and Daniel Callahan, eds, *Abortion: Understanding Differences*, 47–72. New York: Plenum
– 1990a. 'The Family Crisis, the Family Wage and Feminism: Historical and Theoretical Considerations.' In Elshstain, *Power Trips and Other Journeys: Essays in Feminism as Civic Discourse*, 61–72. Madison: University of Wisconsin Press
– 1990b. 'The Family and Civic Life.' In Elshtain, *Power Trips and Other Journeys*, 45–60
Etzioni, Amitai. 1988. *The Moral Dimension: Toward a New Economics.* New York: Free Press
Finch, Janet. 1989. *Family Obligations and Social Change.* Cambridge, Eng.: Polity
Finch, Janet, and D. Groves. 1983. *A Labour of Love: Women, Work and Caring.* London: Routledge and Kegan Paul
Franklin, Bob. 1986. *The Rights of Children.* Oxford: Basil Blackwell
Fraser, Nancy. 1989. 'Women, Welfare, and the Politics of Need Interpretation.' In Fraser, *Unruly Practices: Discourse and Gender in Contemporary Social Theory*, 144–90. Minneapolis: University of Minnesota Press
Freud, Sigmund. 1913/1950. *Totem and Taboo.* London: Routledge and Kegan Paul
Frye, Northrop. 1967. 'The Knowledge of Good and Evil.' In Max Black, ed., *The Morality of Scholarship*, 1–28. Ithaca: Cornell University Press
Galbraith, John Kenneth. 1992. *The Culture of Contentment.* Boston: Houghton Mifflin Company
Gaylin, W., and R. Macklin. 1982. *Who Speaks for the Child: The Problems of Proxy Consent.* New York: Plenum
Gilligan, Carol. 1982. *In a Different Voice: Psychological Theory and Women's Development.* Cambridge: Harvard University Press
Gilligan, Carol, et al. 1988. *Mapping the Moral Domain: A Contribution of Women's Thinking to Psychological Theory and Education.* Cambridge: Harvard University Press
Glendon, Mary Ann. 1989. *The Transformation of Family Law: State,*

Law, and the Family in the United States and Western Europe. Chicago: University of Chicago Press

Glossop, Robert G. 1988. 'Bronfenbrenner's Ecology of Human Development: A Reappreciation.' In Alan R. Pence, eds., *Ecological Research with Children and Families: From Concepts to the Methodology,* 2–15. New York: Teachers College Press

Godbout, Jacques T., and Alain Caille. 1992. *L'esprit du don.* Paris: Editions La Découverte

Goffman, Erving. 1952. 'Cooling the Mark Out: Some Aspects of Adaption to Failure!' *Psychiatry* 15 (November): 451–63

Goodin, Robert E. 1985. *Protecting the Vulnerable: A Reanalysis of Our Social Responsibilities.* Chicago: University of Chicago Press

Gordon, Linda. 1976. *Women's Body, Women's Rights: Birth Control in America.* New York: Grossman

Gough, Ian. 1979. *The Political Economy of the Welfare State.* London: Macmillan

Gouldner, Alvin W. 1960. 'The Norm of Reciprocity: A Preliminary Statement.' *American Sociological Review* 25, no. 2 (April): 161–78.

Grobstein, Clifford. 1988. *Science and the Unborn: Choosing Human Futures.* New York: Basic Books

Hamburg, David A. 1992. *Today's Children: Creating a Future for a Generation in Crisis.* New York: Random House

Hayek, Friedrich. 1960. *The Constitution of Liberty.* London: Routledge and Kegan Paul

Heclo, Hugh. 1986. 'General Welfare and Two American Traditions.' *Political Science Quarterly* 101, no. 2: 179–96

Heidegger, Martin. 1960. *Essays on Metaphysics: Identity and Difference.* New York: Philosophical Library

Held, Virginia. 1987. 'Non-Contractual Society.' In Marsha Hame and Kai Neilsen, eds, *Science, Morality And Feminist Theory,* 111–38. Calgary: University of Calgary Press

Hertzmann, Clyde. 1990. 'Where Are the Differences Which Make a Difference? Thinking about the Determinants of Health.' Canadian Institute for Advanced Research Population Health, Working Paper no. 8. Toronto: CIAR

Hills, John, Howard Glennerster, and Julian Le Grand. 1993. *Investigating Welfare: Final Report of the ESRC Welfare Research Programme.* London: STICERD/WSP/92

Hirsch, Fred. 1977. *Social Limits of Growth.* London: Routledge and Kegan Paul

Holt, John. 1974. *Escape from Childhood.* New York: Ballantine Books

References   125

Hunsley, Terrance. 1992. 'Financing Social Policy in the Global Economy.' Unpublished paper. Kingston: Queen's University School of Policy Studies
Hutchinson, A.C., and L.J.M. Green. 1989. *Law and the Community.* Toronto: Carswell
Ignatieff, Michael. 1984. *The Needs of Strangers.* London: Hogarth Press
Illich, Ivan. 1982. *Gender.* New York: Pantheon Books
Inhelder, B., and Jean Piaget. 1958. *The Growth of Logical Thinking from Childhood to Adolescence.* New York: Basic Books
Institute for Public Policy Research. 1993. *The Justice Gap.* London: IPPR
Jacobs, Jane. 1961. *The Death and Life of Great American Cities.* New York: Vintage Books
Jencks, Christopher, et al. 1972. *Inequality: A Reassessment of the Effect of Family and Schooling in America.* New York: Harper and Row
Johnson, Paul, Christoph Conrad, and David Thomson. 1989. *Workers versus Pensioners: Intergenerational Justice in an Ageing World.* Manchester: Manchester University Press
Jordan, Bill. 1987. *Rethinking Welfare.* Oxford: Basil Blackwell
Keating, Daniel P., and J. Fraser Mustard. 1993. 'Social Economic Factors and Human Development.' In *Family Security in Insecure Times,* 87–105. Ottawa: National Forum on Family Security
Kohlberg, L. 1984. *Essays on Moral Development,* vol. 2, *The Psychology of Moral Development.* San Francisco: Harper and Row
Korpi, Walter. 1983. *The Democratic Class Struggle.* London: Routledge and Kegan Paul
Krüsselburg, Hans-Gunther. 1987. 'Vital Capital Policy and the Unity of the Social Budget.' *International Journal of Sociology* 17, no. 3: 81–97
Laslett, Peter, and James S. Fishkin. 1992. *Justice Between Age Groups and Generations.* New Haven: Yale University Press
Lévi-Strauss, Claude. 1969. *The Elementary Structures of Kinship.* London: Eyre and Spottiswoode
McDaniel, Susan A. 1993. 'Where the Contradictions Meet: Women and Family Security in Canada in the 1990's.' In *Family Security in Insecure Times,* 163–80. Ottawa: National Forum on Family Security
Maciver, R.M. 1920. *Community: A Sociological Study.* London: Macmillan
McKie, Craig. 1993. 'Demographic Change and Quality-of-Life Concerns in Postwar Canada.' In *Family Security in Insecure Times,* 107–34. Ottawa: National Forum on Family Security
Macpherson, C.B. 1962. *The Political Theory of Possessive Individualism: Hobbes to Locke.* Oxford: Clarendon Press

– 1973. *Democratic Theory: Essays in Retrieval.* Oxford: Clarendon Press

Marquand, David. 1988. *The Unprincipled Society: New Demands and Old Politics.* London: Jonathan Cape

Martin, Rex. 1985. *Rawls and Rights.* Lawrence: University Press of Kansas

Marzorati, Gerald, et al. 1991. 'The Origins of Duty.' *Harper's Magazine* (February): 44–54

Mauss, Marcel. 1967. *The Gift: Forms and Functions of Exchange in Archaic Societies.* New York: Norton

Maxwell, Judith. 1993. 'Globalization and Family Security,' In *Family Security in Insecure Times,* Ottawa: National Forum on Family Security

May, William F. 1975. 'Code, Covenant, Contract or Philanthropy.' *Hastings Center Report* 5 (December): 29–38

Meadows, Donella H., et al. 1972. *The Limits to Growth: A Report for the Club of Rome's Project on the Predicament of Mankind.* New York: Universe Books

Merton, Robert King. 1963. 'Social Structure and Anomie.' In Merton, *Social Theory and Social Structure.* New York: Free Press

Mills, C. Wright. 1961. *The Sociological Imagination.* New York: Grove Press

Mingione, Enzo. 1991. *Fragmented Societies: A Sociology of Economic Life beyond the Market Paradigm.* Oxford: Basil Blackwell

Minow, Martha. 1986. 'Rights for the Next Generation: A Feminist Approach to Children's Rights.' *Harvard Women's Law Journal* 9, no. 1: 1–24

Mohr, Hans. 1984. 'The Future of the Family, the Law, and the State.' *Canadian Journal of Family Law* 4: 260–73

Mueller, Dennis C. 1974. 'Intergenerational Justice and the Social Discount Rate.' *Theory and Decision* 5: 263–73.

– Robert D. Tollison, and Thomas D. Willet. 1974. 'The Utilitarian Contract: A Generalization of Rawls' Theory of Justice.' *Theory and Decision* 4: 345–67

Mulhall, Stephen, and Adam Swift. 1992. *Liberals and Communitarians.* Oxford: Blackwell

Muszynski, Leon. 1991. 'Rethinking the Problem of Poverty: The Labour Market and the Welfare State.' 5th Conference on Social Welfare Policy, Bishop's University, Lennoxville, Quebec, 26 August 1991

Neal, Patrick, and David Paris. 1990. 'Liberalism and the Communitarian Critique: A Guide for the Perplexed.' *Canadian Journal of Political Science* 23, no. 3 (September): 419–39

References   127

Nicholson, Linda. 1986. *Gender and History: The Limits of Social Theory in the Age of the Family*. New York: Columbia University Press

O'Connor, James. 1973. *The Fiscal Crisis of the State*. New York: St Martin's Press

Offe, Claus. 1988. 'Democracy against the Welfare State? Structural Foundations of Neoconservative Political Opportunities.' In Donald Moon, ed., *Responsibility, Rights and Welfare: The Theory of the Welfare State*, 189–228. Boulder: Westview Press

O'Neill, John. 1972. *Sociology as a Skin Trade: Essays toward a Reflexive Sociology*. London: Heinemann

– 1982. 'Defamilization and the Feminization of Law in Early and Late Capitalism.' *International Journal of Law and Psychiatry* 5: 255–69

– 1985. *Five Bodies: The Human Shape of Modern Society*. Ithaca: Cornell University Press

– 1989. *The Communicative Body: Studies in Communicative Philosophy, Politics and Sociology*. Evanston: Northwestern University Press

– 1990. 'AIDS as a Globalizing Panic.' In Mike Featherstone, ed., *Global Culture: Nationalism, Globalization and Modernity*, 329–42. London: Sage Publications

– 1991. *Plato's Cave: Desire, Power and the Specular Functions of the Media*. Norwood, NJ: Ablex Publishing

– 1992. *Modes of Individualism and Collectivism*. Aldershot: Gregg Revivals

O'Neill, Onora, and William Ruddick. 1979. *Having Children: Philosophical and Legal Reflections on Parenthood*. New York: Oxford University Press

Osberg, Lars. 1990. 'Distributional Issues and the Future of the Welfare State.' In K. Newton, T. Schweitzer, and J.P. Voyer, *Perspective 2000: Proceedings of a Conference Sponsored by the Economic Council of Canada*, 159–80. Ottawa: Canadian Government Publishing Centre

Pahl, Robert. 1988. 'Some Remarks on Informal Work, Social Polarization and the Social Structure.' *International Journal of Urban and Regional Research* 12, no. 2: 247–67

Pateman, Carole. 1988. *The Sexual Contract*. Oxford: Basil Blackwell

Polyani, Karl. 1944. *The Great Transformation: The Political and Economic Origins of Our Time*. New York: Rinehart and Company

Powell, Lisa M. 1992. 'Toward Child Care Policy Development in Canada.' In Terrance M. Hunsley, ed., *Social Policy in the Global Economy*, 155–82. Kingston: Queen's University School of Policy Studies

Pruger, Robert. 1973. 'Social Policy: Unilateral Transfer or Reciprocal Exchange.' *Journal of Social Policy* 2, no. 4: 289–302

Putnam, Robert D. 1993. 'The Prosperous Community: Social Capital and Public Life.' *The American Prospect* 13 (Spring): 35–42

Rawls, John. 1971. *A Theory of Justice.* Oxford: Oxford University Press

Ressler, Everett M., et al. 1993. *Children in War: A Guide to the Provision of Services.* New York: UNICEF

Roche, Maurice. 1992. *Rethinking Citizenship: Welfare and Change in Modern Society.* Oxford: Blackwell Publishers

Sandel, Michael J. 1982. *Liberalism and the Limits of Justice.* Cambridge: Cambridge University Press

Schoeman, Ferdinand. 1980. 'Rights of Children, Rights of Parents, and the Moral Basis of the Family.' *Ethics* 91 (October): 6–19

Schwarzenbach, Sibyl. 1987. 'Rawls and Ownership: The Forgotten Category of Reproductive Labour.' In Marsja Hame and Kai Nielsen, eds, *Science, Morality and Feminist Theory,* 139–67. Calgary: University of Calgary Press

Shields, Craig. 1993. *Issues in Family Life and Family Support: A Background Paper.* Ontario: Premier's Council on Health, Well-Being and Social Justice

Sinclair, Timothy J. 1993. *Passing Judgment: Credit Rating Processes as Regulatory Mechanisms of Governance in the Emerging World Order.* Toronto: Centre for International and Strategic Studies, York University

Social Well-Being: A Paradigm for Reform. 1993. North York, Ont.: Roeher Institute

Sommers, Christina Hoff. 1986. 'Filial Morality.' *Journal of Philosophy* 83, no. 8: 439–56

Sullivan, Terrance. 1992. *Sexual Abuse and the Rights of Children: Reforming Canadian Law.* Toronto: University of Toronto Press

– 1992. 'Reflections on Children: Politics and the Canadian Constitution.' Unpublished paper prepared for Politics of Childhood and Children at Risk, European Centre for Social Welfare, Kellowski, Finland

Tawney, R.H. 1931/1961. *Equality.* New York: Harcourt, Brace and Co.

Taylor, Charles. 1979. 'Atomism.' In Alkis Kontos, ed., *Powers, Possessions and Freedom: Essays in Honour of C.B. Macpherson,* 39–61. Toronto: University of Toronto Press

Taylor-Gooby, Peter. 1991. *Social Change, Social Welfare and Social Science.* Toronto: University of Toronto Press

Thomson, David. 1991. *Selfish Generations? The Ageing of New Zealand's Welfare State.* Wellington: Bridget Williams Books

Titmuss, R.M. 1970. *The Gift Relationship: From Human Blood to Social Policy.* London: Allen and Unwin

Trakman, Leon E. 1991. *Reasoning with the Charter.* Toronto: Butterworths

Turner, Bryan S. 1986. *Citizenship and Capitalism: The Debate over Citizenship.* London: Allen and Unwin

UNICEF. 1990. *Children and Development in the 1990's: A UNICEF Sourcebook.* New York: United Nations

Valpy, Michael. 1993. 'The Myth of the Myth of Canadian Compassion.' In *Family Security in Insecure Times,* 181–205. Ottawa National Forum on Family Security

Walzer, Michael. 1983. *Spheres of Justice: A Defense of Pluralism and Equality.* New York: Basic Books

Wilson, H.T. 1989. *Sex and Gender: Making Cultural Sense of Civilization.* Leiden: E.J. Brill

– Forthcoming. *The Legitimacy of Capitalism: Public Capital and the Wealth of Nations in Post Industrial Societies*

Wolfe, Alan. 1989. *Whose Keeper? Social Science and Moral Obligation.* Berkeley: University of California Press

Wrong, Dennis H. 1962. 'The Over-Socialized Conception of Man in Modern Sociology.' *Psychoanalysis and the Psychoanalytic Review* 49, no. 2: 53–69

Index

132   Index